The Common Sense of Socialism

by John Spargo

TO

GEORGE H. STROBELL

AS A TOKEN OF FRIENDSHIP AND LOVE THIS LITTLE BOOK IS AFFECTIONATELY
INSCRIBED

CONTENTS

THE COMMON SENSE OF SOCIALISM

I

BY WAY OF INTRODUCTION

Socialism is undoubtedly spreading. It is, therefore, right and expedient that its teachings, its claims, its tendencies, its accusations and promises, should be honestly and seriously examined.--Prof. Flint.

My Dear Mr. Edwards: I count it good fortune to receive such letters of inquiry as that which you have written me. You could not easily have conferred greater pleasure upon me than you have by the charming candor and vigor of your letter. It is said that when President Lincoln saw Walt Whitman, "the good, Gray Poet," for the first time he exclaimed, "Well, he looks like a man!" and in like spirit, when I read your letter I could not help exclaiming, "Well, he writes like a man!"

There was no need, Mr. Edwards, for you to apologize for your letter: for its faulty grammar, its lack of "style" and "polish." I am not insensible to these, being a literary man, but, even at their highest valuation, grammar and literary style are by no means the most important elements of a letter. They are, after all, only like the clothes men wear. A knave or a fool may be dressed in the most perfect manner, while a good man or a sage may be poorly dressed, or even clad in rags. Scoundrels in broadcloth are not uncommon; gentlemen in fustian are sometimes met with.

He would be a very unwise man, you will admit, who tried to judge a man by his coat. President Lincoln was uncouth and ill-dressed, but he was a wise man and a gentleman in the highest and best sense of that much misused word. On the other hand, Mr. Blank, who represents railway interests in the United States Senate, is sleek, polished and well-dressed, but he is neither very wise nor very good. He is a gentleman only in the conventional, false sense of that word.

Lots of men could write a more brilliant letter than the one you have written to me, but there are not many men, even among professional writers, who could write a better one. What I like is the spirit of earnestness and the simple directness of it. You say that you have "Read lots of things in the papers about the Socialists' ideas and listened to some Socialist speakers, but never could get a very clear notion of what it was all about." And then you add "Whether Socialism is good or bad, wise or foolish, I want to know."

I wish, my friend, that there were more working men like you; that there were millions of American men and women crying out: "Whether Socialism is good or bad, wise or foolish, I want to know." For that is the beginning of wisdom: back of all the intellectual progress of the race is the cry, I want to know! It is a cry that belongs to wise hearts, such as Mr. Ruskin meant when he said, "A little group of wise hearts is better than a wilderness full of fools." There are lots of fools, both educated and uneducated, who say concerning Socialism, which is the greatest movement of our time, "I don't know anything about it and I don't want to know anything about it." Compared with the most learned man alive who takes that position, the least educated laborer in the land who says "I want to know!" is a philosopher compared with a fool.

When I first read your letter and saw the long list of your objections and questions I confess that I was somewhat frightened. Most of the questions are fair questions, many of them are wise ones and all of them merit consideration. If you will bear with me, Mr. Edwards, and let me answer them in my own way, I propose to answer them all. And in answering them I shall be as honest and frank with you as I am with my own soul. Whether you believe in Socialism or not is to me a matter of less importance than whether you understand it or not.

You complain that in some of the books written about Socialism there are lots of hard, technical words and phrases which you cannot properly understand, even when you have looked in the dictionary for their meaning, and that is a very just complaint. It is true that most of the books on Socialism and other important subjects are written by students for students, but I shall try to avoid that difficulty and write as a plain, average man of fair sense to another plain, average man of fair sense.

All your other questions and objections, about "stirring up class hatred," about "dividing-up the wealth with the lazy and shiftless," trying to "destroy religion," advocating "free love" and "attacking the family," all these and the many other matters contained in your letter, I shall try to answer fairly and with absolute honesty.

I want to convert you to Socialism if I can, Mr. Edwards, but I am more anxious to have you understand Socialism.

II

WHAT'S THE MATTER WITH AMERICA?

It seems to me that people are not enough aware of the monstrous state of society, absolutely without a parallel in the history of the world, with a population poor, miserable and degraded in body and mind, as if they were slaves, and yet called freemen. The hopes entertained by many of the effects to be wrought by new churches and schools, while the social evils of their conditions are left uncorrected, appear to me utterly wild.--Dr. Arnold, of Rugby.

The working-classes are entitled to claim that the whole field of social institutions should be re-examined, and every question considered as if it now arose for the first time, with the idea constantly in view that the persons who are to be convinced are not those who owe their ease and importance to the present system, but persons who have no other interest in the matter than abstract justice and the general good of the community.--John Stuart Mill.

I presume, Mr. Edwards, that you are not one of those persons who believe that there is nothing the matter with America; that you are not wholly content with existing conditions. You would scarcely be interested in Socialism unless you were convinced that in our existing social system there are many evils for which some remedy ought to be found if possible. Your interest in Socialism arises from the fact that its advocates claim that it is a remedy for the social evils which distress you--is it not so?

I need not harrow your feelings, therefore, by drawing for you pictures of dismal misery, poverty, vice, crime and squalor. As a workingman, living in Pittsburg, you are unhappily familiar with the evils of our present system. It doesn't require a professor of political economy to understand that something is wrong in our American life today.

As an industrial city Pittsburg is a notable example of the defective working of our present social and industrial system. In Pittsburg, as in every other modern city, there are the extremes of wealth and poverty. There are beautiful residences on the one hand and miserable, crowded tenement hovels upon the other hand. There are people who are so rich, whose incomes are so great, that their lives are made miserable and unhappy. There are other people so poor, with incomes so small, that they are compelled to live miserable and unhappy lives. Young men and women, inheritors of vast fortunes, living lives of idleness, uselessness and vanity at one end of the social scale are driven to dissipation and debauchery and crime. At the other end of the social scale there are young men and women, poor, overburdened with toil, crushed by poverty and want, also driven to dissipation and debauchery and crime.

You are a workingman. All your life you have known the conditions which surround the lives of working people like yourself. You know how hard it is for the most careful and industrious workman to properly care for his family. If he is fortunate enough never to be sick, or out of work, or on strike, or to be involved in an accident, or to have sickness in his family, he may become the owner of a cheap home, or, by dint of much sacrifice, his children may be educated and enabled to enter one of the professions. Or, given all the conditions stated, he may be enabled to save enough to provide for himself and wife a pittance sufficient to keep them from pauperism and beggary in their old age.

That is the best the workingman can hope for as a result of his own labor under the very best conditions. To attain that level of comfort and decency he must deny himself and his wife and children of many things which they ought to enjoy. It is not too much to say that none of your fellow-workmen in Pittsburg, men known to you, your neighbors and comrades in labor, have been able to attain such a condition of comparative comfort and security except by dint of much hardship imposed upon themselves, their wives and children. They have had to forego many innocent pleasures; to live in poor streets, greatly to the disadvantage of the children's health and morals; to concentrate their energies to the narrow and sordid aim of saving money; to cultivate the instincts and feelings of the miser.

The wives of such men have had to endure privations and wrongs such as only the wives of the workers in civilized society ever know. Miserably housed, cruelly overworked, toiling incessantly from morn till night, in sickness as well as in health, never knowing the joys of a real vacation, cooking, scrubbing, washing, mending, nursing and pitifully saving, the wife of such a worker is in truth the slave of a slave.

At the very best, then, the lot of the workingman excludes him and his wife and children from most of the comforts which belong to modern civilization. A well-fitted home in a good neighborhood--to say nothing of a home beautiful in itself and its surroundings--is out of the question; foreign travel, the opportunity to enjoy the rest and educative advantages of occasional journeys to other lands, is likewise out of the question. Even though civic enterprise provides public libraries and art galleries, museums, lectures, concerts, and other opportunities of recreation and education, there is not the leisure for their enjoyment to any extent. For our model workman, with all his exceptional advantages, after a day's toil has little time left for such things, and little strength or desire, while his wife has even less time and even less desire.

You know that this is not an exaggerated account. It may be questioned by the writers of learned treatises who know the life of the workers only from descriptions of it written by people who know very little about it, but you will not question it. As a workman you know it is true. And I know it is true, for I have lived it. The best that the most industrious, thrifty, persevering and fortunate workingman can hope for is to be decently housed, decently fed, decently clothed. That he and his family may always be certain of these things, so that they go down to their graves at last without having experienced the pangs of hunger and want, the worker must be exceptionally fortunate. And yet, my friend, the horses in the stables of the rich men of this country, and the dogs in their kennels, have all these things, and more! For they are protected against such overwork and such anxiety as the workingman and the workingman's wife must endure. Greater care is taken of the health of many horses and dogs than the most favored workingman can possibly take of the health of his boys and girls.

At its best and brightest, then, the lot of the workingman in our present social system is not an enviable one. The utmost good fortune of the laboring classes is, properly considered, a scathing condemnation of modern society. There is very little poetry, beauty, joy or glory in the life of the workingman when taken at its very best.

But you know very well that not one workingman in a hundred, nay, not one in a thousand, is fortunate enough never to be sick, or out of work, or on strike, or to be involved in an accident, or to have sickness in his family. Not one worker in a thousand lives to old age and goes down to his grave without having known the pangs of hunger and want, both for himself and those dependent upon him. On the contrary, dull, helpless, poverty is the lot of millions of workers whose lines are cast in less pleasant places.

Mr. Frederic Harrison the well-known conservative English publicist, some years ago gave a graphic description of the lot of the working class of England, a description which applies to the working class of America with equal force. He said:

"Ninety per cent of the actual producers of wealth have no home that they can call their own beyond the end of a week, have no bit of soil, or so much as a room that belongs to them; have nothing of value of any kind except as much as will go in a cart; have the precarious chance of weekly wages which barely suffice to keep them in health; are housed for the most part in places that no man thinks fit for his horse; are separated by so narrow a margin from destruction that a month of bad trade, sickness or unexpected loss brings them face to face with hunger and pauperism."[1]

I am perfectly willing, of course, to admit that, upon the whole, conditions are worse in England than in this country, but I am still certain that Mr. Harrison's description is fairly applicable to the United States of America, in this year of Grace, nineteen hundred and eight.

At present we are passing through a period of industrial depression. Everywhere there are large numbers of unemployed workers. Poverty is rampant. Notwithstanding all that is being done to ease their misery, all the doles of the charitable and compassionate, there are still many thousands of men, women and children who are hungry and miserable. You see them every day in Pittsburg, as I see them in New York, Philadelphia, Boston, Cleveland, Chicago, and elsewhere. It is easy to see in times like the present that there is some great, vital defect in our social economy.

Later on, if you will give me your attention, Jonathan, I want you to consider the causes of such cycles of depression as this that we are so patiently enduring. But at present I am interested in getting you to realize the terrible shortcomings of our industrial system at its best, in normal times. I want to have you consider the state of affairs in times that are called "prosperous" by the politicians, the preachers, the economists, the statisticians and the editors of our newspapers. I am not concerned, here and now, with the exceptional distress of such periods as the present, but with the ordinary, normal, chronic misery and distress; the poverty that is always so terribly prevalent.

Do you remember the talk about the "great and unexampled prosperity" in which you indulged during the latter part of 1904 and the following year? Of course you do. Everybody was talking about prosperity, and a stranger visiting the United States might have concluded that we were a nation of congenital optimists. Yet, it was precisely at that time, in the very midst of our loud boasting about prosperity, that Robert Hunter challenged the national brain and conscience with the statement that there were at lease ten million persons in poverty in the United States. If you have not read Mr. Hunter's book, Jonathan, I advise you to get it and read it. You will find in it plenty of food for serious thought. It is called Poverty, and you can get a copy at the public library. From time to time I am going to suggest that you read various books which I believe you will find useful. "Reading maketh a full man," provided that the reading is seriously and wisely done. Good books relating to the problems you have to face as a worker are far better for reading than the yellow newspapers or the sporting prints, my friend.

When they first read Mr. Hunter's startling statement that there were ten million persons in the United States in poverty, many people thought that he must be a sensationalist of the worst type. It could not be true, they thought. But when they read the startling array of facts upon which that estimate was based they modified their opinion. It is significant, I think, that there has been no very serious criticism of the estimate made by any reputable authority.

Do you know, Jonathan, that in New York of all the persons who die one in every ten dies a pauper and is buried in Potter's Field? It is a pity that we have not statistics upon this point covering most of our cities, including your own city of Pittsburg. If we had, I should ask you to try an experiment. I should ask you to give up one of your Saturday afternoons, or any day when you might be idle, and to take your stand at the busiest corner in the city. There, I would have you count the people as they pass by, hurrying to and fro, and every tenth person you counted I would have you note by making a little cross on a piece of paper. Think what an awful tally it would be, Jonathan. How sick and weary at heart you would be if you stood all day counting, saying as every tenth person passed, "There goes another marked for a pauper's grave!" And it might happen, you know, that the fateful count of ten would mark your own boy, or your own wife.

We are a practical, hard-headed people. That is our national boast. You are a Yankee of the good old Massachusetts stock, I understand, proud of the fact that you can trace your descent right back to the Pilgrim Fathers. But with all our hard-headed practicality, Jonathan, there is still some sentiment left in us. Most of us dread the thought of a pauper's grave for ourselves or friends, and struggle against such fate as we struggle against death itself. It is a foolish sentiment perhaps, for when the soul leaves the body a mere handful of clod and marl, the spark of divinity forever quenched, it really does not matter what happens to the body, nor where it crumbles into dust. But we cherish the sentiment, nevertheless, and dread having to fill pauper graves. And when ten per cent, of those who die in the richest city of the richest nation on earth are laid at last in pauper graves and given pauper burial there is something radically and cruelly wrong.

And you and I, with our fellows, must try to find out just what the wrong is, and just how we can set it right. Anything less than that seems to me uncommonly like treason to the republic, treason of the worst kind. Alas! Alas! such treason is very common, friend Jonathan--there are many who are heedless of the wrongs that sap the life of the republic and careless of whether or no they are righted.

FOOTNOTES:

[1] Report of the Industrial Remuneration Conference, 1886, p. 429.

III

THE TWO CLASSES IN THE NATION

Mankind are divided into two great classes--the shearers and the shorn. You should always side with the former against the latter.--Talleyrand.

All men having the same origin are of equal antiquity; nature has made no difference in their formation. Strip the nobles naked and you are as well as they; dress them in your rags, and you in their robes, and you will doubtless be the nobles. Poverty and riches only discriminate betwixt you.--Machiavelli.

Thou shalt not steal. Thou shalt not be stolen from.--Thomas Carlyle.

I want you to consider, friend Jonathan, the fact that in this and every other civilized country there are two classes. There are, as it were, two nations in every nation, two cities in every city. There is a class that lives in luxury and a class that lives in poverty. A class constantly engaged in producing wealth but owning little or none of the wealth produced and a class that enjoys most of the wealth without the trouble and pain of producing it.

If I go into any city in America I can find beautiful and costly mansions in one part of the city, and miserable, squalid tenement hovels in another part. And I never have to ask where the workers live. I know that the people who live in the mansions don't produce anything; that the wealth producers alone are poor and miserably housed.

Republican and Democratic politicians never ask you to consider such things. They expect you to let them do all the thinking, and to content yourself with shouting and voting for them. As a Socialist, I want you to do some thinking for yourself. Not being a politician, but a simple fellow-citizen, I am not interested in having you vote for anything you do not understand. If you should offer to vote for Socialism without understanding it, I should beg you not to do it. I want you to vote for Socialism, of course, but not unless you know what it means, why you want it and how you expect to get it. You see, friend Jonathan, I am perfectly frank with you, as I promised to be.

You will remember, I hope, that in your letter to me you made the objection that the Socialists are constantly stirring up class hatred, setting class against class. I want to show you now that this is not true, though you doubtless believed that it was true when you wrote it. I propose to show you that in this great land of ours there are two great classes, the "shearers and the shorn," to adopt Talleyrand's phrase. And I want you to side with the shorn instead of with the shearers, because, if I am not sadly mistaken, my friend, you are one of the shorn. Your natural interests are with the workers, and all the workers are shorn and robbed, as I shall try to show you.

You work in one of the great steel foundries of Pittsburg, I understand. You are paid wages for your work, but you have no other interest in the establishment. There are lots of other men working in the same place under similar conditions. Above you, having the authority to discharge you if they see fit, if you displease them or your work does not suit them, are foremen and bosses. They are paid wages like yourself and your fellow workmen. True, they get a little more wages, and they live in consequence in a little better homes than most of you, but they do not own the plant. They, too, may be discharged by other bosses above them. There are a few of the workmen who own a small number of shares of stock in the company, but not enough of them to have any kind of influence in its management. They are just as likely to be turned out of employment as any of you.

Above all the workers and bosses of one kind and another there is a general manager. Wonderful stories are told of the enormous salary he gets. They say that he gets more for one week than you or any of your fellow workmen get for a whole year. You used to know him well when you were boys together. You went to the same school; played "hookey" together; bathed in the creek together. You used to call him "Richard" and he always used to call you "Jon'thun." You lived close to each other on the same street.

But you don't speak to each other nowadays. When he passes through the works each morning you bend to your work and he does not notice you.

Sometimes you wonder if he has forgotten all about the old days, about the games you used to play up on "the lots," the "hookey" and the swimming in the creek. Perhaps he has not forgotten: perhaps he remembers well enough, for he is just a plain human being like yourself Jonathan; but if he remembers he gives no sign.

Now, I want to ask you a few plain questions, or, rather, I want you to ask yourself a few plain questions. Do you and your old friend Richard still live on the same street, in the same kind of houses like you used to? Do you both wear the same kind of clothes, like you used to? Do you and he both go to the same places, mingle with the same company, like you used to in the old days? Does your wife wear the same kind of clothes than his wife does? Does his wife work as hard as your wife does? Do they both belong to the same social "set" or does the name of Richard's wife appear in the Social Chronicle in the daily papers while your wife's does not? When you go to the theater, or the opera, do you and your family occupy as good seats as Richard and his family in the same way that you and he used to occupy "quarter seats" in the gallery? Are your children and Richard's children dressed equally well? Your fourteen-year-old girl is working as a cash-girl in a store and your fifteen-year-old boy is working in a factory. What about Richard's children? They are about the same age you know: is his girl working in a store, his boy in a factory? Richard's youngest child has a nurse to take care of her. You saw her the other day, you remember: how about your youngest child--has she a nurse to care for her?

Ah, Jonathan! I know very well how you must answer these questions as they flash before your mind in rapid succession. You and Richard are no longer chums; your wives don't know each other; your children don't play together, but are strangers to one another; you have no friends in common now. Richard lives in a mansion, while you live in a hovel; Richard's wife is a fine "lady" in silks and satins, attended by flunkeys, while your wife is a poor, sickly, an 鎚 ic, overworked drudge. You still live in the same city, yet not in the same world. You would not know how to act in Richard's home, before all the servants; you would be embarrassed if you sat down at his dinner table. Your children would be awkward and shy in the presence of his children, while they would scorn to introduce your children to their friends.

You have drifted far apart, you two, my friend. Somehow there yawns between you a great, impassable gulf. You are as far apart in your lives as prince and pauper, lord and serf, king and peasant ever were in the world's history. It is wonderful, this chasm that yawns between you. As Shakespeare has it:

Strange it is that bloods Alike of colour, weight and heat, pour'd out together, Would quite confound distinction, yet stand off In differences so mighty.

I am not going to say anything against your one-time friend who is now a stranger to you and the lord of your life. I have not one word to say against him. But I want you to consider very seriously if the changes we have noted are the only changes that have taken place in him since the days when you were chums together. Have you forgotten the Great Strike, when you and your fellow workers went out on strike, demanding better conditions of labor and higher wages? Of course you have not forgotten it, for that was when your scanty savings were all used up, and you had to stand, humiliated and sorrowful, at the relief station, or in the "Bread Line," to get food for your little family.

Those were the dark days when your dream of a little cottage in the country, with hollyhocks and morning-glories and larkspurs growing around it, melted away like the mists of the morning. It was the dream of your young manhood and of your wife's young womanhood; it was the dream of your earliest years together, and you both worked and saved for that little cottage in the suburbs where you would spend the sunset hours of life together. The Great Strike killed your beautiful dream; it killed your wife's hopes. You have no dream now and no hope for the sunset hours. When you think of them you become bitter and try to banish the thought. I know all about that faded dream, Jonathan.

Why did you stay out on strike and suffer? Why did you not remain at work, or at least go back as soon as you saw how hard the fight was going to be? "What! desert my comrades, and be a traitor to my brothers in the fight?" you say. But I thought you did not believe in classes! I thought you were opposed to the Socialists because they set class to fight class! You were fighting the company then, weren't you; trying to force them to give you decent conditions? You called it a fight, Jonathan, and the newspapers, you remember, had great headlines every day about the "Great Labor War."

It wasn't the Socialists who urged you to go out on strike, Jonathan. You had never heard of Socialism then, except once you read something in the papers about some Socialists who were shot down by the Czar's Cossacks in the streets of Warsaw. You got an idea then that a Socialist was a desperado with a firebrand in one hand and a bomb in the other, madly seeking to burn palaces and destroy the lives of rich men and rulers. No, it was not due to Socialist agitation that you went out on strike.

You went out on strike because you had grown desperate on account of the wanton, wicked, needless waste of human life that went on under your very eyes, day after day. You saw man after man maimed, man after man killed, through defects in the machinery, and the company, through your old chum and playmate, refused to make the changes necessary. They said that it would "cost too much money," though you all knew that the shareholders were reaping enormous profits. Added to that, and the fact that you went hourly in dread of similar fate befalling you, your wife had a hard time to make both ends meet. There was a time when you could save something every week, but for some time before the strike there was no saving. Your wife complained; your comrades said that their wives complained. Finally you all agreed that you could stand it no longer; that you would send a committee to interview the manager and tell him that, unless you got better wages and unless something was done to make your lives safer you would go out on strike.

When you and the manager were chums together he was a kind, good-hearted, generous fellow, and you felt certain that when the Committee explained things it would be all right. But you were mistaken. He cursed at them as though they were dogs, and you could scarcely believe your own ears. Do you remember how you spoke to your wife about it, about "the change in Dick"?

You went out on strike. The manager scoured the country for men to take your places. Ruffianly men came from all parts of the country; insolent, strife-provoking thugs. More than once you saw your fellow-workmen attacked and beaten by thugs, and then the police were ordered to club and arrest--not the aggressors but your comrades. Then the manager asked the mayor to send for the troops, and the mayor did as he was bidden do. What else could he do when the leading stockholders in the company owned and controlled the Republican machine? So the Republican mayor wired to the Republican Governor for soldiers and the soldiers came to intimidate you and break the strike. One day you heard a rifle's sharp crack, followed by a tumult and they told you that one of your old friends, who used to go swimming with you and Richard, the manager, had been shot by a drunken sentry, though he was doing no harm.

You were a Democrat. Your father had been a Democrat and you "just naturally growed up to be one." As a Democrat you were very bitter against the Republican mayor and the Republican Governor. You honestly thought that if there had been a good Democrat in each of those offices there would have been no soldiers sent into the city; that your comrade would not have been murdered. You spoke of little else to your fellows. You nursed the hope that at the next election they would turn out the Republicans and put the Democrats in.

But that delusion was shattered like all the rest, Jonathan, when, soon after, the Democratic President you were so proud of, to whom you looked up as to a modern Moses, sent federal troops into Illinois, over the protest of the Governor of that Commonwealth, in defiance of the laws of the land, in violation of the sacred Constitution he had sworn to protect and obey. Your faith in the Democratic Party was shattered. Henceforth you could not trust either the Republican Party or the Democratic Party.

I don't want to discuss the strike further. That is all ancient history to you now. I have already gone a good deal farther afield than I wanted to do, or than I intended to do when I began this letter. I want to go back--back to our discussion of the great gulf that divides you and your former chum, Richard.

I want you to ask yourself, with perfect candor and good faith, whether you believe that Richard has been so much better than you, either as workman, citizen, husband or father, that his present position can be regarded as a just reward for his virtue and ability? I'll put it another way for you, Jonathan: in your own heart do you believe that you are so much inferior to him as a worker or as a citizen, so much inferior in mentality and in character that you deserve the hard fate which has come to you, the ill-fortune compared to his good fortune? Are you and your family being punished for your sins, while he and his family are being rewarded for his virtues? In other words, Jonathan, to put the matter very plainly, do you believe that God has ordained your respective states in accordance with your just deserts?

You know that is not the case, Jonathan. You know very well that both Richard and yourself share the frailties and weaknesses of our kind. Infinite mischief has been done by those who have given the struggle between the capitalists and the workers the aspect of a conflict between "goodness" on the one side and "wickedness" upon the other. Many things which the capitalists do appear very wicked to the workers, and many things which the workers do, and think perfectly proper and right, the capitalists honestly regard as improper and wrong.

I do not deny that there are some capitalists whose conduct deserves our contempt and condemnation, just as there are some workingmen of whom the same is true. Still less would I deny that there is a very real ethical measure of life; that some conduct is anti-social while other conduct is social. I simply want you to catch my point that we are creatures of our environment,

Jonathan; that if the workers and the capitalists could change places, there would be a corresponding change in their views of many things. I refuse to flatter the workers, my friend: they have been flattered too much already.

Politicians seeking votes always tell the workers how greatly they admire them for their intelligence and for their moral excellencies. But you know and I know that they are insincere; that, for the most part, their praise is lying hypocrisy. They practice what you call "the art of jollying the people" because that is an important part of their business. The way they talk to the working class is very different from the way they talk of the working class among themselves. I've heard them, my friend, and I know how most of them despise the workers.

The working men and women of this country have many faults and failings. Many of them are ignorant, though that is not quite their own fault. Many a workingman starves and pinches his wife and little ones to gamble, squandering his money, yes, and the lives of his family, upon horse races, prize-fights, and other brutal and senseless things called "sport." It is all wrong, Jonathan, and we know it. Many of our fellow workmen drink, wasting the children's bread-money and making beasts of themselves in saloons, and that is wrong, too, though I do not wonder at it when I think of the hells they work in, the hovels they live in and the dull, soul-deadening grind of their daily lives. But we have got to struggle against it, got to conquer the bestial curse, before we can get better conditions. Men who soak their brains in alcohol, or who gamble their children's bread, will never be able to make the world a fit place to live in, a place fit for little children to grow in.

But the worst of all the failings of the working class, in my humble judgment, is its indifference to the great problems of life. Why is it, Jonathan, that I can get tens of thousands of workingmen in Pittsburg or any large city excited and wrought to feverish enthusiasm over a brutal and bloody prize-fight in San Francisco, or about a baseball game, and only a man here and there interested in any degree about Child Labor, about the suffering of little babies? Why is it that the workers, in Pittsburg and every other city in America, are less interested in getting just conditions than in baseball games from which all elements of honest, manly sport have been taken away; brutal slugging matches between professional pugilists; horseraces conducted by gamblers for gamblers; the sickening, details of the latest scandal among the profligate, idle rich?

I could get fifty thousand workingmen in Pittsburg to read long, disgusting accounts of bestiality and vice more easily than I could get five hundred to read a pamphlet on the Labor Problem, on the wrongfulness of things as they are and how they might be made better. The masters are wiser, Jonathan. They watch and guard their own interests better than the workers do.

If you owned the tools with which you work, my friend, and whatever you could produce belonged to you, either to use or to exchange for the products of other workers, there would be some reason in your Fourth of July boasting about this

Blest land of Liberty.

But you don't. You, and all other wage-earners, depend upon the goodwill and the good judgment of the men who own the land, the mines, the factories, the railways, and practically all other means of producing wealth for the right to live. You don't own the raw material, the machinery or the railways; you don't control your own jobs. Most of you don't even own your own miserable homes. These things are owned by a small class of, people when their number is compared with the total population. The workers produce the wealth of this and every other country, but they do not own it. They get just enough to keep them alive and in a condition to go on producing wealth--as long as the master class sees fit to have them do it.

Most of the capitalists do not, as capitalists, contribute in any manner to the production of wealth. Some of them do render services of one kind and another in the management of the industries they are connected with. Some of them are directors, for example, but they are always paid for their services before there is any distribution of profits. Even when their "work" is quite perfunctory and useless, mere make-believe, like the games of little children, they get paid far more than the actual workers. But there are many people who own stock in the company you work for, Jonathan, who never saw the foundries, who were never in the city of Pittsburg in their lives, whose knowledge of the affairs of the company is limited to the stock quotations in the financial columns of the morning papers.

Think of it: when you work and produce a dollar's worth of wealth by your labor, it is divided up. You get only a very small fraction. The rest is divided between the landlords and the capitalists. This happens in the case of every man among the thousands employed by the company. Only a small share goes to the workers, a third, or a fourth, perhaps, the remainder being divided among people who have done none of the work. It may happen, does happen in fact, that, an old profligate whose delight is the seduction of young girls, a wanton woman whose life would shame the harlot of the streets, a lunatic in an asylum, or a baby in the cradle, will get more than any of the workers who toil before the glaring furnaces day after day.

These are terrible assertions, Jonathan, and I do not blame you if you doubt them. I shall prove them for you in a later letter.

At present, I want you to get hold of the fact that the wealth produced by the workers is so distributed that the idle and useless classes get most of it. People will tell you, Jonathan, that "there are no classes in America," and that the Socialists lie when they say so. They point out to you that your old chum, Richard, who is now a millionaire, was a poor boy like yourself. They say he rose to his present position because he had keener brains than his fellows, but you know lots of workmen in the employ of the company who know a great deal more about the work than he does, lots of men who are cleverer than he is. Or they tell you that he rose to his present position because of his superior character, but you know that he is, to say the least, no better than the average man who works under him.

The fact is, Jonathan, the idle capitalists must have some men to carry on the work for them, to direct it and see that the workers are exploited properly. They must have some men to manage things for them; to see that elections are bought, that laws in their interests are passed and not laws in the interests of the people. They must have somebody to do the things they are too "respectable" to do--or too lazy. They take such men from the ranks of the workers and pay them enormous salaries, thereby making them members of their own class. Such men are really doing useful and necessary work in managing the business (though not in corrupting legislators or devising swindling schemes) and are to that extent producers. But their interests are with the capitalists. They live in palaces, like the idlers; they mingle in the same social sets; they enjoy the same luxuries. And, above all, they can invest part of their large incomes in other concerns and draw enormous profits from the labors of other toilers, sometimes even in other lands. They are capitalists and their whole influence is on the side of the capitalists against the workers.

I want you to think over these things, friend Jonathan. Don't be afraid to do your own thinking! If you have time, go to the library and get some good books on the subject and read them carefully, doing your own thinking no matter what the authors of the books may say. I suggest that you get W.J. Ghent's Mass and Class to begin with. Then, when you have read that, I shall be glad to have you read Chapter VI of a book called Socialism: A Summary and Interpretation of Socialist Principles. It is not very hard reading, for I wrote the book myself to meet the needs of just such earnest, hard-working men as yourself.

I think both books will be found in the public library. At any rate, they ought to be. But if not, it would be worth your while to save the price of a few whiskies and to buy them for yourself. You see, Jonathan, I want you to study.

IV

HOW WEALTH IS PRODUCED AND HOW IT IS DISTRIBUTED

It is easy to persuade the masses that the good things of this world are unjustly divided--especially when it happens to be the exact truth.--J.A. Froude.

The growth of wealth and of luxury, wicked, wasteful and wanton, as before God I declare that luxury to be, has been matched step by step by a deepening and deadening poverty, which has left whole neighborhoods of people practically without hope and without aspiration.--Bishop Potter.

At present, all the wealth of Society goes first into the possession of the Capitalist.... He pays the landowner his rent, the labourer his wages, the tax and tithe-gatherer their claims, and keeps a large, indeed, the largest, and a constantly augmenting share of the annual produce of labour for himself. The Capitalist may now be said to be the first owner of all the wealth of the community, though no law has conferred on him the right of this property.... This change has been effected by the taking of interest on Capital ... and it is not a little curious that all the lawgivers of Europe endeavoured to prevent this by Statutes--viz., Statutes against usury.--Rights of Natural and Artificial Property Contrasted (An Anonymous work, published in London, in 1832).--Th. Hodgskin.

You are not a political economist, Jonathan, nor a statistician. Most books on political economy, and most books filled with statistics, seem to you quite unintelligible. Your education never included the study of such books and they are, therefore, almost if not quite worthless to you.

But every working man ought to know something about political economy and be familiar with some statistics relating to social conditions. So I am going to ask you to study a few figures and a little political economy. Only just a very little, mind you, just to get you used to thinking about social problems in a scientific way. I think I can set the fundamental principles of political economy before you in very simple language, and I will try to make the statistics interesting.

But I want to warn you again, Jonathan, that you must use your own commonsense. Don't trust too much to theories and figures--especially figures. Somebody has said that you can divide the liars of the world into three classes--liars, damned liars and statisticians. Some people are paid big salaries for juggling with figures to fool the American people into believing what is not true, Jonathan. I want you to consider the laws of political economy and all the statistics I put before you in the light of your own commonsense and your own practical experience.

Political economy is the name which somebody long ago gave to the formal study of the production and distribution of wealth. Carlyle called it "the dismal science," and most books on the subject are dismal enough to justify the term. Upon my library shelves there are some hundreds of volumes dealing with political economy, and I don't mind confessing to you that some of them I never have been able to understand, though I have put no little effort and conscience into the attempt. I have a suspicion that the authors of these books could not understand them themselves. That the reason why they could not write so that a man of fair intelligence and education could understand them was the fact that they had no clear ideas to convey.

Now, in the first place, what do we mean by Wealth? Why, you say, wealth is money and money is wealth. But that is only half true, Jonathan. Suppose, for example, that an American millionaire crossing the ocean be shipwrecked and find himself cast upon some desert island, like another Robinson Crusoe, without food or means of obtaining any. Suppose him naked, without tool or weapon of any kind, his one sole possession being a bag containing ten thousand dollars in gold and banknotes to the value of as many millions. With that money, in New York, or any other city in the world, he would be counted a rich man, and he would have no difficulty in getting food and clothing.

But alone upon that desert island, what could he do with the money? He could not eat it, he could not keep himself warm with it? He would be poorer than the poorest savage in Africa whose only possessions were a bow and arrow and an assegai, or spear, wouldn't he? The poor kaffir who never heard of money, but who had the simple weapons with which to hunt for food, would be the richer man of the two, wouldn't he?

I think you will find it useful, Jonathan, to read a little book by John Ruskin, called Unto This Last. It is a very small book, written in very simple and beautiful language. Mr. Ruskin was a somewhat whimsical writer, and there are some things in the book which I do not wholly agree with, but upon the whole it is sane, strong and eternally true. He shows very clearly, according to my notion, that the mere possession of things, or of money, is not wealth, but that wealth consists in the possession of things useful to us. That is why the possession of heaps of gold by a man living alone upon a desert island does not make him wealthy, and why Robinson Crusoe, with weapons, tools and an abundant food supply, was really a wealthy man, though he had not a dollar.

In a primitive state of society, then, he is poor who has not enough of the things useful to him, and he who has them in abundance is rich, or wealthy.

Note that I say this of "A primitive state of society," Jonathan, for that is most important. It is not true of our present capitalist state of society. This may seem a strange proposition to you at first, but a little careful thought will convince you that it is true.

Consider a moment: Mr. Carnegie is a wealthy man and Mr. Rockefeller is a wealthy man. They are, each of them, richer than most of the princes and kings whose wealth astonished the ancient world. Mr. Carnegie owns shares in many companies, steelmaking companies, railway companies, and so on. Mr. Rockefeller, owns shares in the Standard Oil Company, in railways, coal mines, and so on. But Mr. Carnegie does not personally use any of the steel ingots made in the works in which he owns shares. He uses practically no steel at all, except a knife or two. Mr. Rockefeller does not use the oil-wells he owns, nor a hundred-millionth part of the coal his shares in coal-mines represent.

If one could get Mr. Carnegie into one of the works in which he is interested and stand with him in front of one of the great furnaces as it poured forth its stream of molten metal, he might say: "See! that is partly mine. It is part of my wealth!" Then, if one were to ask "But what are you going to do with that steel, Mr. Carnegie--is it useful to you?" Mr. Carnegie would laugh at the thought. He would probably reply, "No, bless your life! The steel is useless to me. I don't want it. But somebody else does. It is useful to other people."

Ask Mr. Rockefeller, "Is this oil refinery your property, Mr. Rockefeller?" and he would reply: "It is partly mine. I own a big share in it and it represents part of my wealth." Ask him next: "But, Mr. Rockefeller, what are you going to do with all that oil? Surely, you cannot need so much oil for your own use?" and he, like Mr. Carnegie, would reply: "No! The oil is useless to me. I don't want it. But somebody else does. It is useful to other people."

To be rich in our present social state, Jonathan, you must not only own an abundance of things useful to you, but also things useful only to others, which you can sell to them at a profit. Wealth, in our present society, then consists in the possession of things having an exchange value--things which other people will buy from you. So endeth our first lesson in political economy.

And here beginneth our second lesson, Jonathan. We must now consider how wealth is produced.

The Socialists say that all wealth is produced by labor applied to natural resources. That is a very simple answer, which you can easily remember. But I want you to examine it well. Think it over: ask yourself whether anything in your experience as a workingman confirms or disproves it. Do you produce wealth? Do your fellow workers produce wealth? Do you know of any other way in which wealth can be produced than by labor applied to natural resources? Don't be fooled, Jonathan. Think for yourself!

The wealth of a fisherman consists in an abundance of fish for which there is a good market. But suppose there is a big demand for fish in the cities and that, at the same time, there are millions of fish in the sea, ready to be caught. So long as they are in the sea, the fish are not wealth. Even if the sea belonged to a private individual, as the oil-wells belong to Mr. Rockefeller and a few other individuals, nobody would be any the better off. Fish in the sea are not wealth, but fish in the market-places are. Why, because labor has been expended in catching them and bringing them to market.

There are millions of tons of coal in Pennsylvania. President Baer said, you will remember, that God had appointed him and a few other gentlemen to look after that coal, to act as His trustees. And Mr. Baer wasn't joking, either. That is the funny part of the story: he was actually serious when he uttered that foolish blasphemy! There are also millions of people who want coal, whose very lives depend upon it. People who will pay almost any price for it rather than go without it.

The coal is there, millions of tons of it. But suppose that nobody digs for it; that the coal is left where Nature produced it, or where God placed it, whichever description you prefer? Do you think it would do anybody any good lying there, just as it lay untouched when the Indian roved through the forests ignorant of its presence? Would anybody be wealthier on account of the coal being there? Of course not. It only becomes wealth when somebody's labor makes it available. Every dollar of the wealth of our coal-mining industry, as of the fishing industries, represents human labor.

I need not go through the list of all our industries, Jonathan, to make this truth clear to you. If it pleases you to do so, you can easily do that for yourself. I simply wanted to make it clear that the Socialists are stating a great universal truth when they say that labor applied to natural resources is the true source of all wealth. As Sir William Petty said long ago: "Labor is the father and land is the mother of all wealth."

But you must be careful, Jonathan, not to misuse that word "labor."

Socialists don't mean the labor of the hands only, when they speak of labor. Take the case of the coal-mines again, just for a moment: There are men who dig the coal, called miners. But before they can work there must be other men to make tools and machinery for them. And before there can be machinery made and fixed in its proper place there must be surveyors and engineers, men with a special education and capacity, to draw the plans, and so on. Then there must be some men to organize the business, to take orders for the coal, to see that it is shipped, to collect the payment agreed upon, so that the workers can be paid, and so on through a long list of things requiring mental labor.

Both kinds of labor are equally necessary, and no one but a fool would ever think otherwise. No Socialist writer or lecturer ever said that wealth was produced by manual labor alone applied to natural resources. And yet, I hardly ever pick up a book or newspaper article written against Socialism in which that is not charged against the Socialists! The opponents of Socialism all seem to be lineal descendants of Ananias, Jonathan!

For your special, personal benefit I want to cite just one instance of this misrepresentation. You have heard, I have no doubt, of the English gentleman, Mr. W.H. Mallock, who came to this country last year to lecture against Socialism. He is a very pleasant fellow, personally--as pleasant a fellow as a confirmed aristocrat who does not like to ride in the street cars with "common people" can be. Mr. Mallock was hired by the Civic Federation and paid out of funds which Mr. August Belmont contributed to that body, funds which did not belong to Mr. Belmont, as the investigation of the affairs of the New York Traction Companies conducted later by the Hon. W.M. Ivins, showed. He was hired to lecture against Socialism in our great universities and colleges, in the interests of people like Mr. Belmont. And there was not one of those universities or colleges fair enough to say: "We want to hear the Socialist side of the argument!" I don't think the word "fairplay," about which we used to boast as one of the glories of our language, is very much liked or used in American universities, Jonathan. And I am very sorry. It ought not to be so.

I should have been very glad to answer Mr. Mallock's silly and unjust attacks; to say to the professors and students in the universities and colleges: "I want you to listen to our side of the argument and then make up your minds whether we are right or whether truth is on the side of Mr. Mallock." That would have been fair and honest and manly, wouldn't it? There were several other Socialist lecturers, the equals of Mr. Mallock in education and as public speakers, who would have been ready to do the same thing. And not one of us would have wanted a cent of anybody's money, let alone money contributed by Mr. August Belmont.

Mr. Mallock said that the Socialists make the claim that manual labor alone creates wealth when applied to natural objects. That statement is not true. He even dared say that a great and profound thinker like Karl Marx believed and taught that silly notion. The newspapers of America hailed Mr. Mallock as the long-looked-for conqueror of Marx and his followers. They thought he had demolished Socialism. But did they know that they were resting their case upon a lie, I wonder? That Marx never for a moment believed such a thing; that he went out of his way to explain that he did not?

I don't want you to try to read the works of Marx, my friend--at least, not yet: Capital, his greatest work, is a very difficult book, in three large volumes. But if you will go into the public library and get the first volume in English translation, and turn to page 145, you will read the following words:

"By labor power or capacity for labor is to be understood the aggregate of those mental and physical capabilities existing in a human being, which he exercises when he produces a use-value of any description."[2]

I think you will agree, Jonathan, that that statement fully justifies all that I have said concerning Mr. Mallock. I think you will agree, too, that it is a very clear and intelligible definition, which any man of fair sense can understand. Now, by way of contrast, I want you to read one of Mr. Mallock's definitions. Please bear in mind that Mr. Mallock is an English "scholar," by many regarded as a very clear thinker. This is how he defines labor:

"Labor means the faculties of the individual applied to his own labor."

I have never yet been able to find anybody who could make sense out of that definition, Jonathan, though I have submitted it to a good many people, among them several college professors. It does not mean anything. The fifty-seven letters contained in that sentence would mean just as much if you put them in a bag, shook them up, and then put them on paper just as they happened to fall out of the bag. Mr. Mallock's English, his veracity and his logic are all equally weak and defective.

I don't think that Mr. Mallock is worthy of your consideration, Jonathan, but if you are interested in reading what he said about Socialism in the lectures I have been referring to, they are published in a volume entitled, A Critical Examination of Socialism. You can get the book in the library: they will be sure to have it there, because it is against Socialism. But I want you to buy a little book by Morris Hillquit, called Mr. Mallock's "Ability," and read it carefully. It costs only ten cents--and you will get more amusement reading the careful and scholarly dissection of Mallock than you could get in a dime show anywhere. If you will read my own reply to Mr. Mallock, in my little book Capitalist and Laborer, I shall not think the worse of you for doing so.

Now, let us look at the division of the wealth. It is all produced by labor of manual workers and brain workers applied to natural objects which no man made. I am not going to weary you with figures, Jonathan, because you are not a statistician. I am going to take the statistics and make them as simple as I can for you--and tell you where you can find the statistics if you ever feel inclined to try your hand upon them.

But first of all I want you to read a passage from the writings of a very great man, who was not a "wicked Socialist agitator" like your humble servant. Archdeacon Paley, the great English theologian, was not like many of our modern clergymen, afraid to tell the truth about social conditions; he was not forgetful of the social aspects of Christ's teaching. Among many profoundly wise utterances about social conditions which that great and good teacher made more than a century ago was the passage I now want you to read and ponder over. You might do much worse than to commit the whole passage to memory. It reads:

"If you should see a flock of pigeons in a field of corn, and if (instead of each picking where and what it liked, taking just as much as it wanted, and no more) you should see ninety-nine of them gathering all they got into a heap, reserving nothing for themselves but the chaff and the refuse, keeping this heap for one, and that the weakest, perhaps worst, pigeon of the flock, sitting round and looking on, all the winter, whilst this one was devouring, throwing about and wasting it; and if a pigeon, more hardy or hungry than the rest, touched a grain of the hoard, all the others instantly flying upon it, and tearing it to pieces; if you should see this, you would see nothing more than what is every day practised and established among men.

"Among men you see the ninety-and-nine toiling and scraping together a heap of superfluities for one (and this one, too, oftentimes the feeblest and worst of the set, a child, a woman, a madman or a fool), getting nothing for themselves, all the while, but a little of the coarsest of the provision which their own industry produces; looking quietly on, while they see the fruits of all their labor spent or spoiled; and if one of their number take or touch a particle of the hoard, the others joining against him, and hanging him for theft."

If there were many men like Dr. Paley in our American churches to-day, preaching the truth in that fearless fashion, there would be something like a revolution, Jonathan. The churches would no longer be empty almost; preachers would not be wondering why workingmen don't go to church. There would probably be less show and pride in the churches; less preachers paid big salaries, less fashionable choirs. But the churches would be much nearer to the spirit and standard of Jesus than most of them are to-day. There is nothing in connection with modern religious life quite so glaring as the infidelity of the Christian ministry to the teachings of Christ.

A lady once addressed Thomas Carlyle concerning Jesus in this fashion: "How delighted we should all be to throw open our doors to him and listen to his divine precepts! Don't you think so, Mr. Carlyle?" The bluff old puritan sage answered: "No, madam, I don't. I think if he had come fashionably dressed, with plenty of money, and preaching doctrines palatable to the higher orders, I might have had the honor of receiving from you a card of invitation, on the back of which would be written, 'To meet our Saviour.' But if he came uttering his sublime precepts, and denouncing the pharisees, and associating with publicans and the lower orders, as he did, you would have treated him as the Jews did, and cried out, 'Take him to Newgate and hang him.'"

I sometimes wonder, Jonathan, what really would happen if the Carpenter-preacher of Gallilee could and did visit some of our American churches. Would he be able to stand the vulgar show? Would he be able to listen in silence to the miserable perversion of his teachings by hired apologists of social wrong? Would he want to drive out the moneychangers and the Masters of Bread, to hurl at them his terrible thunderbolts of wrath and scorn? Would he be welcomed by the churches bearing his name? Would they want to listen to his gospel? Frankly, Jonathan, I doubt it. A few Socialists would be found in nearly every church ready to receive him and to call him "Comrade," but the majority of church-goers would shun him and pass him by.

I should not be surprised, Jonathan, if the President of the United States called him an "undesirable citizen," as he surely would call Archdeacon Paley if he were alive.

I wanted you to read Paley's illustration of the pigeons before going into the unequal distribution of wealth. It will help you to understand another illustration. Suppose that from a shipwreck one hundred men are fortunate enough to save themselves and to make their way to an island, where, making the best of conditions, they establish a little community, which they elect to call "Capitalia." Luckily, they have all got food and clothing enough to last them for a little while, and they are fortunate enough to find on the island a supply of tools, evidently abandoned by some former occupants of the island.

They set to work, cultivating the ground, building huts for themselves, hunting for game, and so on. They start out to face the primeval struggle with the sullen forces of Nature as our ancestors did in the time long past. Their efforts prosper, every one of the hundred men being a worker, every man working with equal will, equal strength and vigor. Now, then, suppose that one day, they decide to divide up the wealth produced by their labor, to institute individual property in place of common property, competition in place of co-operation. What would you think if two or three of the strongest members said, "We will do the dividing, we will distribute the wealth according to our ideas of justice and right," and then proceeded to give 55 per cent. of the wealth to one man, to the next eleven men 32 per cent. and to the remaining eighty-eight men only 13 per cent. between them?

I will put it in another way, Jonathan, since you are not accustomed to thinking in percentages. Suppose that there were a hundred cows to be divided among the members of the community. According to the scheme of division just described, this is how the division would work out:

1 Man would get 55 Cows for himself 11 Men would get 32 Cows among them 88 Men would get 13 Cows among them

When they had divided the cows in this manner they would proceed to divide the wheat, the potato crops, the land, and everything else owned by the community in the same unequal way. I ask you again, Jonathan, what would you think of such a division?

Of course, being a fair-minded man, endowed with ordinary intelligence at least, you will admit that there would be no sense and no justice in such a plan of division, and you doubt if intelligent human beings would submit to it.

But, my friend, that is not quite so bad as the distribution of wealth in America to-day is. Suppose that instead of all the members of the little island community being workers, all working equally hard, fairly sharing the work of the community, one man absolutely refused to do anything at all, saying, "I was the first one to get ashore. The land really belongs to me. I am the landlord. I won't work, but you must work for me." And suppose that eleven other men said in like manner. "We won't work. We found the tools, we brought the seeds and the food out of the boats when we came. We are the capitalists and you must do the work in the fields. We will superintend you, give you orders where to dig, and when, and where to stop. You eighty-eight common fellows are the laborers who must do the hard work while we use our brains." And suppose that they actually carried out that plan and then divided the wealth in the way I have described, that would be a pretty good illustration of how the wealth produced in America under our existing social system is divided.

And I ask you what you think of that, Jonathan Edwards. How do you like it?

These are not my figures. They are not the figures of any rabid Socialist making frenzied guesses. They are taken from a book called The Present Distribution of Wealth in the United States, by the late Dr. Charles B. Spahr, a book that is used in most of our colleges and universities. No serious criticism of the figures has ever been attempted and most economists, even the conservative ones, base their own estimates upon Spahr's work. It would be worth your while to get the book from the library, Jonathan, and to read it carefully.

In the meantime, look over the following table which sets forth the results of Dr. Spahr's investigation, Jonathan, and remember that the condition of things has not improved since 1895, when the book was written, but that they have, on the contrary, very much worsened.

SPAHR'S TABLE OF THE DISTRIBUTION OF WEALTH IN THE UNITED STATES

==========+=============+=======+==========+=================+==
===== | No. of | Per | Average | Aggregate | Per Class | Families | Cent |
Wealth | Wealth | Cent ----------+------------+-------+----------+----------------+-------
Rich | 125,000 | 1.0 | $263,040 | 32,880,000,000 | 54.8 Middle | 1,362,500 |
10.9 | 14,180 | 29,320,000,000 | 32.2 Poor | 4,762,500 | 38.1 | 1,639 |
7,800,000,000 | 13.0 Very Poor | 6,250,000 | 50.0 | | | ----------+------------+----
---+----------+------------------+------- Total | 13,500,000 | 100.0 | $4,800 |
$60,000,000,000 | 100.0 ----------+------------+-------+----------+----------------+-----
--

Now, Jonathan, although I have taken a good deal of trouble to lay these figures before you, I really don't care very much for them. Statistics don't impress me as they do some people, and I would far rather rely upon your commonsense than upon any figures. I have not quoted these figures because they were published by a very able scholar in a very wise book, nor because scientific men, professors of political economy and others, have accepted them as a fair estimate. I have used them because I believe them to be true and reliable.

But don't you rest your whole faith upon them, Jonathan. If some fine day a Republican spellbinder, or a Democratic scribbler, tries to upset you and prove that Socialists are all liars and false prophets, just tell him the figures are quite unimportant to you, that you don't care to know just exactly how much of the wealth the richest one per cent. gets and how little of it the poorest fifty per cent. gets. A few millions more or less don't trouble you. Pin him down to the one fact which your own commonsense teaches you, that the wealth of the country is unequally distributed. Tell him that you know, regardless of figures, that there are many idlers who are enormously rich and many honest, industrious workers who are miserably poor. He won't be able to deny these things. He dare not, because they are true.

Ask any such apologist for capitalism what he would think of the father or mother who took his or her eight children and said: "Here are eight cakes, as many cakes as there are boys and girls. I am going to distribute the cakes. Here, Walter, are seven of the cakes for you. The other cake the rest of you can divide among yourselves as best you can." If the capitalist defender is a fair-minded man, if he is neither fool nor liar nor monster, he will agree that such a parent would be brutally unjust.

Yet, Jonathan, that is exactly how our national wealth is divided up. One-eighth of the families in the United States do get seven-eights of the wealth, and, being, I hope, neither fool, liar nor monster, I denounce the system as brutally unjust. There is no sense and no morality in mincing matters and being afraid to call spades spades.

It is because of this unjust distribution of the wealth of modern society that we have so much social unrest. That is the heart of the whole problem. Why are workingmen organized into unions to fight the capitalists, and the capitalists on their side organized to fight the workers? Why, simply because the capitalists want to continue exploiting the workers, to exploit them still more if possible, while the workers want to be exploited less, want to get more of what they produce.

Why is it that eminently respectable members of society combine to bribe legislators--to buy laws from the lawmakers!--and to corrupt the republic, a form of treason worse than Benedict Arnold's? Why, for the same reason: they want to continue the spoliation of the people. That is why the heads of a great life insurance company illegally used the funds belonging to widows and orphans to contribute to the campaign fund of the Republican Party in 1904. That is why, also, Mr. Belmont used the funds of the traction company of which he is president to support the Civic Federation, which is an organization specially designed to fool and mislead the wage-earners of America. That is why every investigation of American political or business life that is honestly made by able and fearless men reveals so much chicanery and fraud.

You belong to a union, Jonathan, because you want to put a check upon the greed of the employers. But you never can expect through the union to get all that rightfully belongs to you. It is impossible to expect that the union will ever do away with the terrible inequalities in the distribution of wealth. The union is a good thing, and the workers ought to be much more thoroughly organized into unions than they are. Socialists are always on the side of the union when it is engaged in an honest fight against the exploiters of labor.

Later on, I shall take up the question of unionism and discuss it with you, Jonathan. Meanwhile, I want to impress upon your mind that a wise union man votes as he strikes. There is not the least bit of sense in belonging to a union if you are to become a "scab" when you go to the ballot-box. And a vote for a capitalist party is a scab vote, Jonathan.

FOOTNOTES:

[2] Note: In the American edition, published by Kerr, the page is 186.

V

THE DRONES AND THE BEES

Hitherto it is questionable if all the mechanical inventions yet made have lightened the day's toil of any human being. They have enabled a greater population to live the same life of drudgery and imprisonment, and an increased number of manufactures, and others, to make large fortunes.--John Stuart Mill.

Most people imagine that the rich are in heaven, but as a rule it is only a gilded hell. There is not a man in the city of New York with brains enough to own five millions of dollars. Why? The money will own him. He becomes the key to a safe. That money will get him up at daylight; that money will separate him from his friends; that money will fill his heart with fear; that money will rob his days of sunshine and his nights of pleasant dreams. He becomes the property of that money. And he goes right on making more.

What for? He does not know. It becomes a kind of insanity.--R.G. Ingersoll.

Is it well that, while we range with Science, glorying in the time, City children soak and blacken soul and sense in City slime? There, among the gloomy alleys, Progress halts on palsied feet, Crime and Hunger cast our maidens by the thousand on the street. There the master scrimps his haggard seamstress of her daily bread, There a single sordid attic holds the living and the dead; There the smouldering fire of fever creeps across the rotted floor, In the crowded couch of incest, in the warrens of the poor. --Tennyson.

When you and I were boys going to school, friend Jonathan, we were constantly admonished to study with admiration the social economy of the bees. We learned to almost reverence the little winged creatures for the manner in which they

Improve each shining hour, And gather honey all the day From every opening flower.

We were taught, you remember, to honor the bees for their hatred of drones. It was the great virtue of the bees that they always drove the drones from the hive. For my part, I learned the lesson so well that I really became a sort of bee-worshipper. But since I have grown to mature years I have come to the conclusion that those old lessons were not honestly meant, Jonathan. For if anybody proposes to-day that we should drive out the drones from the human hive, he is at once denounced as an Anarchist and an "undesirable citizen."

It is all very well for bees to insist that there must be no idle parasites, that the drones must go, but for human beings such a policy won't do! It savors too much of Socialism, my friend, and is unpleasantly like Paul's foolish saying that "If any man among you will not work, neither shall he eat." That is a text which is out of date and unsuited to the twentieth century!

"Allah! Allah!" cried the stranger, "Wondrous sights the traveller sees; But the greatest is the latest, Where the drones control the bees!"

Every modern civilized nation rewards its drones better than it rewards its bees, and in every land the drones control the bees.

I want you to consider, friend Jonathan, the lives of the people. How the workers live and how the shirkers live; now the bees live and how the drones live, if you like that better. You can study the matter for yourself, right in Pittsburg, much better than you can from books, for God knows that in Pittsburg there are the extremes of wealth and poverty, just as there are in New York, Chicago, St. Louis or San Francisco. There are gilded hells where rich drones live and squalid hells where poor bees live, and the number of truly happy people is sadly, terribly, small.

Ten millions in poverty! Don't you think that is a cry so terrible that it ought to shame a great nation like this, a nation more bounteously endowed by Nature than any other nation in the world's history? Men, women and children, poor and miserable, with not enough to eat, nor clothes to keep them warm in the cold winter nights; with places for homes that are unfit for dogs, and these not their own; knowing not if to-morrow may bring upon them the last crushing blow. All these conditions, and conditions infinitely worse than these, are contained in the poverty of those millions, Jonathan.

If people were poor because the land was poor, because the country was barren, because Nature dealt with us in niggardly fashion, so that all men had to struggle against famine; if, in a word, there was democracy in our poverty, so that none were idle and rich while the rest toiled in poverty, it would be our supreme glory to bear it with cheerful courage. But that is not the case. While babies perish for want of food and care in dank and unhealthy hovels, there are pampered poodles in palaces, bejeweled and cared for by liveried flunkies and waiting maids. While men and women want bread, and beg crusts or stand shivering in the "bread lines" of our great cities, there are monkeys being banqueted at costly banquets by the profligate degenerates of riches. It's all wrong, Jonathan, cruelly, shamefully, hellishly wrong! And I for one, refuse to call such a brutalized system, or the nation tolerating it, civilized.

Good old Thomas Carlyle would say "Amen!" to that, Jonathan. Lots of people wont. They will tell you that the poverty of the millions is very sad, of course, and that the poor are to be pitied. But they will remind you that Jesus said something about the poor always being with us. They won't read you what he did say, but you can read it for yourself. Here it is: "For ye have the poor always with you, and whensoever ye will ye can do them good."[3] And now, I want you to read a quotation from Carlyle:

"It is not to die, or even to die of hunger, that makes a man wretched; many men have died; all men must die,--the last exit of us all is in a Fire-Chariot of Pain. But it is to live miserable we know not why; to work sore and yet gain nothing; to be heart-worn, weary, yet isolated, unrelated, girt-in with a cold universal Laissezfaire: it is to die slowly all our life long, imprisoned in a deaf, dead, Infinite Injustice, as in the accursed iron belly of a Phalaris' Bull! This is and remains forever intolerable to all men whom God has made."

"Miserable we know not why"--"to die slowly all our life long"--"Imprisoned in a deaf, dead, Infinite Injustice"--Don't these phrases describe exactly the poverty you have known, brother Jonathan?

Did you ever stop to think, my friend, that poverty is the lot of the average worker, the reward of the producers of wealth, and that only the producers of wealth are poor? Do you know that, because we die slowly all our lives long, the death-rate among the working-class is far higher than among other classes by reason of overwork, anxiety, poor food, lack of pleasure, bad housing, and all the other ills comprehended in the lot of the wage-worker? In Chicago, for example, in the wards where the well-to-do reside the death-rate is not more than 12 per thousand, while it is 37 in the tenement districts.

Scientists who have gone into the matter tell us that of ten million persons belonging to the well-to-do classes the annual deaths do not number more than 100,000, while among the very best paid workers the number is not less than 150,000 and among the very poorest paid workers at least 350,000. To show you just what those proportions are, I have represented the matter in a little diagram, which you can understand at a glance:

There are some diseases, notably the Great White Plague. Consumption, which we call "diseases of the working-classes" on account of the fact that they prey most upon the wearied, ill-nourished bodies of the workers. Not that they are confined to the workers entirely, but because the workers are most afflicted by them. Because the workers live in crowded tenement hovels, work in factories laden with dust and disease germs, are overworked and badly fed, this and other of the great scourges of the human race find them ready victims.

Marble and stone cutters. 540 Cigar makers and tobacco workers. 476 Compositors, printers, pressmen. 435 Barbers and hairdressers. 334 Masons (brick and stone). 294 Iron and steel workers. 236 Physicians and Surgeons. 168 Engineers and Surveyors. 145 School teachers. 144 Lawyers. 140 Clergymen. 123 Bankers, brokers, officials of companies, etc. 92]

I want you to study this diagram and the figures by which it is accompanied, Jonathan. You will observe that the death rate from Consumption among marble and stone cutters is six times greater than among bankers and brokers and directors of companies. Among cigar makers and tobacco workers it is more than five times as great. Iron and steel workers do not suffer so much from the plague as some other workers, according to the death-rates. One reason is that only fairly robust men enter the trade to begin with. Another reason is that a great many, finding they cannot stand the strain, after they have become infected, leave the trade for lighter occupations. I think there can be no doubt that the true mortality from Consumption among iron and steel workers is much higher than the figures show. But, taking the figures as they are, confident that they understate the extent of the ravages of the disease in these occupations, we find that the mortality is more than two and a half times greater than among capitalists.

Now, these are very serious figures, Jonathan. Why is the mortality so much less among the capitalists? It is because they have better homes, are not so overworked to physical exhaustion, are better fed and clothed, and can have better care and attention, far better chances of being cured, if they are attacked. They can get these things only from the labor of the workers, Jonathan.

In other words, they buy their lives with ours. Workers are killed to keep capitalists alive.

It used to be frequently charged that drink was the chief cause of the poverty of the workers; that they were poor because they were drunken and thriftless. But we hear less of that silly nonsense than we used to, though now and then a Prohibitionist advocate still repeats the old and long exploded myth. It never was true, Jonathan, and it is less true to-day than ever before. Drunkenness is an evil and the working class suffers from it to a lamentable degree, but it is not the sole cause of poverty, it is not the chief cause of poverty, it is not even a very important cause of poverty at all.

It is true that intemperance causes poverty in some cases, it is also true that drunkenness is very frequently caused by poverty. They act and react upon each other, but it is not doubted by any student of our social conditions whose opinion carries any weight that intemperance is far more often the result of poverty and bad conditions of life and labor than the cause of them.

The International Socialist Congress which met at Stuttgart last summer very rightly decided that Socialists everywhere should do all in their power to combat alcoholism, to end the ravages of intemperance among the working classes of all nations. For drunken voters are not very likely to be either wise or free voters: we need sober, earnest, clear-thinking men to bring about better conditions, Jonathan. But the Socialists, while they adopt this position, do not mistake results for causes. They know from actual experience that Solomon was right when he attributed intemperance to ill conditions. Hunt out your Bible and turn to the Book of Proverbs, chapter 31, verse 7. There you will read: "Let him drink and forget his poverty, and remember his misery no more."

That is not very good advice to give a workingman, but it is exactly what many workingmen do. There was a wise English bishop who said a few years ago that if he lived in the slums of any of the great cities, under conditions similar to those in which most of the workers live, he would probably be a drunkard, and when I see the conditions under which millions of men are working and living I wonder that we have not more drunkenness than we have.

A good many years ago, "General" Booth, head of the Salvation Army, declared that "nine-tenths" of the poverty of the people was due to intemperance. Later on, "Commissioner" Cadman, one of the "General's" most trusted aides, made an investigation of the causes of poverty among all those who passed through the Army shelters for destitute men and women. He found that among the very lowest class, the "submerged tenth," where the ravages of drink are most sadly evident, depression in trade counted for much more than drink as a cause of poverty. The figures were:

Depression in trade 55.8 per cent. Drink and Gambling 26.6 per cent. Ill-health 11.6 per cent. Old Age 5.8 per cent.

Even among the very lowest class of the social wrecks of our great cities, who have long since abandoned hope, depression in trade was found to count for more than twice as much as drink and gambling combined as a producer of poverty.

That is in keeping with all the investigations that have ever been made in a scientific spirit. Professor Amos Warner, in his valuable study of the subject, published in his book, American Charities, shows how false the notion that nearly all the poverty of the people is due to their intemperance proves to be when an intelligent investigation of the facts is made.

Dr. Edward T. Devine, of Columbia University, editor of Charities and the Commons, is probably as competent an authority upon this question as any man living. He is not likely to be called a Socialist by anybody. Yet I find him writing in his magazine, at the end of November, 1907: "The tradition which many hold that the condition of poverty is ordinarily and as a matter of course to be explained by personal faults of the poor themselves is no longer tenable. Strong drink and vice are abnormal, unnatural and essentially unattractive ways of spending surplus income." Dr. Devine very frankly and bravely admits that poverty is an unnecessary evil, "a shocking, loathsome excrescence on the body politic, an intolerable evil which should come to an end." What else, indeed, could a sane man think of it?

As a conservative man, I say without reservation that accidents incurred in the course of employment, and sickness brought on by industrial conditions, such as overwork accompanied by under nourishment, exposure to extremes of temperature, unsanitary workshops and factories and the inhalation of contaminated atmosphere, are far more important causes of poverty among the workers than intemperance. Every investigation ever made goes to prove this true. I wish that every one who seeks to blame the poverty of the poor upon the victims themselves would study a few facts, which I am going to ask you to study, without prejudice or passion. They would readily see then how false the belief is.

Last year there was a Committee of very expert investigators in New York which made a careful inquiry into the relation of wages to the standard of living. They were not Socialists, these gentlemen, or I should not submit their testimony. I am anxious to base my case against our present social system upon evidence that is not in any way biased in favor of Socialism. Dr. Lee K. Frankel was Chairman of the Committee. He is Director of the United Hebrew Charities of New York City, an able and sincere man, but not a Socialist. Dr. Devine, another able and sincere man who is by no means a Socialist, was a member of the Committee. Among the other members were also such persons as Bishop Greer, of New York, Reverend Adolph Guttman, president of the Hebrew Relief Society, Syracuse, New York, Mrs. William Einstein, president of Emanu El Sisterhood, New York; Mr. Homer Folks, Secretary State Charities Aid Association and Reverend William J. White, of Brooklyn, Supervisor of Catholic Charities. The Committee was deputed to make the investigation by the New York State Conference of Charities and Corrections, and made its report in November, 1907, at Albany, N.Y.

I think you will agree, Jonathan, that it would be very hard to imagine a more conservative body, less inoculated with the virus of Socialism than that. From their report to the Conference I note that the Committee reported that as a result of their work, after going carefully into the expenditure of some 322 families, they had come to the conclusion that the lowest amount upon which a family of five could be supported in decency and health in New York City was about eight hundred dollars a year. I am quite sure, Jonathan, that there is not one of the members of that Committee who would think that even that sum would be enough to keep their families in health and decency; not one who would want to see their children living under the best conditions which that sum made possible. They were philanthropists you see, Jonathan, "figuring out" how much the "Poor" ought to be able to live on. And to help them out they got Professor Chapin, of Beloit College and Professor Underhill, of Yale. Professor Underhill being an expert physiological chemist, could advise them as to the sufficiency of the expenditures upon food among the families reported.

But the total income of thousands of families falls very short of eight hundred dollars a year. There are many thousands of families in which the breadwinner does not earn more than ten dollars a week at best. Making allowance for time lost through sickness, holidays, and so on, it is evident that the total income of such families would not exceed four hundred and fifty dollars a year at best. Even the worker with twenty dollars a week, if there is a brief period of sickness or unemployment, will find himself, despite his best efforts, on the wrong side of the line, compelled either to see his family suffer want or to become dependent on "that cold thing called Charity." And Dr. Devine, writing in Charities and the Commons, admits that the charitable societies cannot hope to make up the deficit, to add to the wages of the workers enough to raise their standards of living to the point of efficiency. He admits that "such a policy would tend to financial bankruptcy."

Taking the unskilled workers in New York City, the vast army of laborers, it is certain that they do not average $400 a year, so that they are, as a class, hopelessly, miserably poor. It is true that many of them spend part of their miserable wages on drink, but if they did not, they would still be poor; if every cent went to buy the necessities of existence, they would still be hopelessly, miserably poor.

The Massachusetts Bureau of Statistics showed a few years ago, when the cost of living was less than now, that a family of five could not live decently and in health upon less than $754 a year, but more than half of the unskilled workers in the shoe-making industry of that State got less than $300 a year. Of course, some were single and not a few were women, but the figures go far to show that the New York conditions are prevalent in New England also. Mr. John Mitchell said that in the anthracite district of Pennsylvania it was impossible to maintain a family of five in decency on less than $600 a year, but according to Dr. Peter Roberts, who is one of the most conservative of living authorities upon the conditions of industry in the coal mines of Pennsylvania, the average wage in the anthracite district is less than $500 and that about 60 per cent. receive less than $450 a year.

I am not going to bother you with more statistics, Jonathan, for I know you do not like them, and they are hard to remember. What I want you to see is that, for many thousands of workers, poverty is an inevitable condition. If they do not spend a cent on drink; never give a cent to the Church or for charity; never buy a newspaper; never see a play or hear a concert; never lose a day's wages through sickness or accident; never make a present of a ribbon to their wives or a toy to their children--in a word, if they live as galley slaves, working without a single break in the monotony and drudgery of their lives, they must still be poor and endure hunger, unless they can get other sources of income. The mother must go out to work and neglect her baby to help out; the little boys and girls must go to work in the days when they ought to be in school or in the fields at play, to help out the beggars' pittance which is their portion. The greatest cause of poverty is low wages.

Then think of the accidents which occur to the wage-earners, making them incapable of earning anything for long periods, or even permanently. At the same meeting of the New York State Conference of Charities and Corrections as that already referred to, there were reports presented by many of the charitable organizations of the state which showed that this cause of poverty is a very serious one, and one that is constantly increasing. In only about twenty per cent. of the accidents of a serious nature investigated was there any settlement made by the employers, and from a list that is of immense interest I take just a few cases as showing how little the life of the average workingman is valued at:

Nature of Injury. Settlement

Spine injured $ 20 and doctor Legs broken 300 Death 100 Death 65 Two ribs broken 20 Paralysis 12 Brain affected 60 Fingers amputated 50

The reports showed that about half of the accidents occurred to men under forty years of age, in the very prime of life. The wages were determined in 241 cases and it was shown that about 25 per cent. were earning less than $10 a week and 60 per cent. were earning less than $15 a week. Even without the accidents occurring to them these workers and their families must be miserably poor, the accidents only plunging them deeper into the frightful abyss of despair, of wasting life and torturous struggle.

No, my friend, it is not true that the poverty of the poor is due to their sins, thriftlessness and intemperance. I want you to remember that it is not the wicked Socialist agitators only who say this. I could fill a book for you with the conclusions of very conservative men, all of them opposed to Socialism, whose studies have forced them to this conclusion.

There was a Royal Commission appointed in England some years ago to consider the problem of the Aged Poor and how to deal with it. Of that Royal Commission Lord Aberdare was chairman--and he was a most implacable enemy of Socialism. The Commission reported in 1895: "We are confirmed in our view by the evidence we have received that ... as regards the great bulk of the working classes, during their lives, they are fairly provident, fairly thrifty, fairly industrious and fairly temperate." But they could not add that, as a result of these virtues, they were also fairly well-to-do! The Right Honorable Joseph Chamberlain, another enemy of Socialism, signed with several others a Minority Report, but they agreed "that the imputation that old age pauperism is mainly due to drink, idleness, improvidence, and the like abuses applies to but a very small proportion of the working population."

Very similar was the report of a Select Committee of the House of Commons, appointed to consider the best means of improving the condition of the "aged and deserving poor." The report read: "Cases are too often found in which poor and aged people, whose conduct and whose whole career has been blameless, industrious and deserving, find themselves from no fault of their own, at the end of a long and meritorious life, with nothing but the workhouse or inadequate outdoor relief as the refuge for their declining years."

And what is true of England in this respect is equally true of America.

Let me repeat here that I am not defending intemperance. I believe with all my heart that we must fight intemperance as a deadly enemy of the working class. I want to see the workers sober; sober enough to think clearly, sober enough to act wisely. Before we can get rid of the evils from which we suffer we must get sober minds, friend Jonathan. That is why the Socialists of Europe are fighting the drink evil; that is why, too, the Prussian Government put a stop to the "Anti-Alcohol" campaign of the workers, led by Dr. Frolich, of Vienna. Dr. Frolich was not advocating Socialism. He was simply appealing to the workers to stop making beasts of themselves, to become sober so that they could think clearly with brains unmuddled by alcohol. And the Prussian

Government did not want that: they knew very well that clear thinking and sober judgment would lead the workers to the ballot boxes under Socialist banners.

I care most of all for the suffering of the innocent little ones. When I see that under our present system it is necessary for the mother to leave her baby's cradle to go into a factory, regardless of whether the baby lives or dies when it is fed on nasty and dangerous artificial foods or poor, polluted milk, I am stirred to my soul's depths. When I think of the tens of thousands of little babies that die every year as a result of these conditions I have described; of the millions of children who go to school every day underfed and neglected, and of the little child toilers in shops, factories and mines, as well as upon the farms, though their lot is less tragic than that of the little prisoners of the factories and mines--I cannot find words to express my hatred of the ghoulish system.

I should like you to read, Jonathan, a little pamphlet on Underfed School Children, which costs ten cents, and a bigger book, The Bitter Cry of the Children, which you can get at the public library. I wrote these to lay before thinking men and women some of the terrible evils from which our children suffer. I know that the things written are true. Every line of them was written with the single purpose of telling the truth as I had seen it.

I made the terrible assertions that more than eighty thousand babies are slain by poverty in America each year; that some "2,000,000 children of school age in the United States are the victims of poverty which denies them common necessities, particularly adequate nourishment"; that there were at least 1,750,000 children at work in this country. These statements, and the evidence given in support of them, attracted widespread attention, both in this country and in Europe. They were cited in the U.S. Senate and in Europe parliaments. They were preached about from thousands of pulpits and discussed from a thousand platforms by politicians, social reformers and others.

A committee was formed in New York City to promote the physical welfare of school children. Although one of the first to take the matter up, I was not asked to serve on that committee, on account of the fact, as I was afterwards told, of my being a Socialist. Well, that Committee, composed entirely of non-Socialists, and including some very bitter opponents of Socialism, made an investigation of the health of school children in New York City. They examined, medically, some 1,400 children of various ages, living in different parts of the city and belonging to various social classes. If the results they discovered are common to the whole of the United States, the conditions are in every way worse than I had declared them to be.

If the conditions found by the medical investigators for this committee are representative of the whole of the United States, then we have not less than twelve million school children in the United States suffering from physical defects more or less serious, and not less than 1,248,000 suffering from malnutrition--from insufficient nourishment, generally due to poverty, though not always--to such an extent that they need medical attention.[4]

Do you think a nation with such conditions existing at its very heart ought to be called a civilized nation? I don't. I say that it is a brutalized nation, Jonathan!

And now I want you to look over a list of another kind of shameful social conditions--a list of some of the vast fortunes possessed by men who are not victims of poverty, but of shameful wealth. I take the list from the dryasdust pages of The Congressional Record, December 12, 1907, from a speech by the Hon. Jeff Davis, United States Senator from Arkansas. I cannot find in the pages of The Congressional Record that it made any impression upon the minds of the honorable senators, but I hope it will make some impression upon your mind, my friend. It is a good deal easier to get a human idea into the head of an honest workingman than into the head of an honorable senator!

Don't be frightened by a few figures. Read them. They are full of human interest. I have put before you some facts relating to the shameful poverty of the workers and their pitiable condition, and now I want to put before you some facts relating to the pitiable condition of the non-workers. I want you to feel some pity for the millionaires!

THE RICHEST FIFTY-ONE IN THE UNITED STATES.

"When the average present-day millionaire is bluntly asked to name the value of his earthly possessions, he finds it difficult to answer the question correctly. It may be that he is not willing to take the questioner into his confidence. It is doubtful whether he really knows.

"If this is true of the millionaire himself, it follows that when others attempt the task of estimating the amount of his wealth the results must be conflicting. Still, excellent authorities are not lacking on this subject, and the list of the richest fifty-one persons in the United States has been satisfactorily compiled.

"The following list is taken from Munsey's Scrap Book of June, 1906, and is a fair presentation of the property owned by fifty-one of the very richest men of the United States.

Rank	Name.	How Made.	Total Fortune.
1	John D. Rockefeller	Oil	$600,000,000
2	Andrew Carnegie	Steel	300,000,000
3	W.W. Astor	Real Estate	300,000,000
4	J. Pierpont Morgan	Finance	150,000,000
5	William Rockefeller	Oil	100,000,000
6	H.H. Rogers	do	100,000,000
7	W.K. Vanderbilt	Railroads	100,000,000
8	Senator Clark	Copper	100,000,000
9	John Jacob Astor	Real Estate	100,000,000
10	Russell Sage	Finance	80,000,000
11	H.C. Frick, Jr.	Steel and Coke	80,000,000
12	D.O. Mills	Banker	75,000,000
13	Marshall Field, Jr.	Inherited	75,000,000
14	Henry M. Flagler	Oil	60,000,000
15	J.J. Hill	Railroads	60,000,000
16

John D. Archbold | Oil | 50,000,000 17 | Oliver Payne | do | 50,000,000 18 | J.B. Haggin | Gold | 50,000,000 19 | Harry Field | Inherited | 50,000,000 20 | James Henry Smith | do | 40,000,000 21 | Henry Phipps | Steel | 40,000,000 22 | Alfred G. Vanderbilt | Railroads | 40,000,000 23 | H.O. Havemeyer | Sugar | 40,000,000 24 | Mrs. Hetty Green | Finance | 40,000,000 25 | Thomas F. Ryan | do | 40,000,000 26 | Mrs. W. Walker | Inherited | 35,000,000 27 | George Gould | Railroads | 35,000,000 28 | J. Ogden Armour | Meat | 30,000,000 29 | E.T. Gerry | Inherited | 30,000,000 30 | Robert W. Goelet | Real Estate | 30,000,000 31 | J.H. Flager | Finance | 30,000,000 32 | Claus Spreckels | Sugar | 30,000,000 33 | W.F. Havemeyer | do | 30,000,000 34 | Jacob H. Schiff | Banker | 25,000,000 35 | P.A.B. Widener | Street Cars | 25,000,000 36 | George F. Baker | Banker | 25,000,000 37 | August Belmont | Finance | 20,000,000 38 | James Stillman | Banker | 20,000,000 39 | John W. Gates | Finance | 20,000,000 40 | Norman B. Ream | do | 20,000,000 41 | Joseph Pulitzer | Journalist | 20,000,000 42 | James G. Bennett | Journalist | 20,000,000 43 | John G. Moore | Finance | 20,000,000 44 | D.G. Reid | Steel | 20,000,000 45 | Frederick Pabst | Brewer | 20,000,000 46 | William D. Sloane | Inherited | 20,000,000 47 | William B. Leeds | Railroads | 20,000,000 48 | James P. Duke | Tobacco | 20,000,000 49 | Anthony N. Brady | Finance | 20,000,000 50 | George W. Vanderbilt | Railroads | 20,000,000 51 | Fred W. Vanderbilt | do | 20,000,000 | | +--------------- | Total | | $3,295,000,000 -----+----------------------+----------------+----------------

"It will thus be seen that fifty-one persons in the United States, with a population of nearly 90,000,000 people, own approximately one thirty-fifth of the entire wealth of the United States. The Statistical Abstract of the United States, 29th number, 1906, prepared under the direction of the Secretary of Commerce and Labor of the United States, gives the estimated true value of all property in the United States for that year at $107,104,211,917.

"Each of the favored fifty-one owns a wealth of somewhat more than $64,600,000, while each of the remaining 89,999,950 people get $1,100. No one of these fifty-one owns less than $20,000,000, and no one on the average owns less than $64,600,000. Men owning from $1,000,000 to $20,000,000 are no longer called rich men. There are approximately 4,000 millionaires in the United States, but the aggregate of their holdings is difficult to obtain. If all their holdings be deducted from the total true value of all the property in the United States, the average share of each of the other 89,995,000 people would be less than $500.

"John Jacob Astor is reputed to have been the first American millionaire, although this is a matter impossible to decide. It is also claimed that Nicholas Longworth, of Cincinnati, the great grandfather of Congressman Longworth, was the first man west of the Allegheny Mountains to amass a million. It is difficult to prove either one of these propositions, but they prove that the age of the millionaire in the United States is a comparatively recent thing. In 1870 to own a single million was to be a very rich man; in 1890 it required at least $10,000,000, while to-day a man with a single million or even ten millions is not in the swim. To be enumerated as one of the world's richest men you must own not less than $20,000,000."

I am perfectly serious when I suggest that the slaves of riches are just as much to be pitied as the slaves of poverty. No man need envy Mr. Rockefeller, for example, because he has something like six hundred millions of dollars, an annual income of about seventy-two millions. He does not own those millions, Jonathan, but they own him. He is a slave to his possessions. If he owns a score of automobiles he can only use one at a time; if he spends millions in building palatial residences for himself he cannot get greater comfort than the man of modest fortune. He cannot buy health nor a single touch of love for money.

Many of our great modern princes of industry and commerce are good men. It is a wild mistake to imagine that they are all terrible ogres and monsters of iniquity. But they are victims of an unjust system. Millions roll into their coffers while they sleep, and they are oppressed by the burden of responsibilities. If they give money away at a rate calculated to ease them of the burdens beneath which they stagger they can only do more harm than good. Mr. Carnegie gives public libraries with the lavishness with which travellers in Italy sometimes throw small copper coins to the beggars on the streets, but he is only pauperising cities wholesale and hindering the progress of real culture by taking away from civic life the spirit of self-reliance. If the people of a small town came together and said: "We ought to have a library in our town for our common advantage: let us unite and subscribe funds for a hundred books to begin with," that would be an expression of true culture.

But when a city accepts a library at Mr. Carnegie's hands, there is an inevitable loss of self-respect and independence. Mr. Carnegie's motives may be good and pure, but the harm done to the community is none the less great.

Mr. Rockefeller may give money to endow colleges and universities from the very highest motives, but he cannot prevent the endowments from influencing the teaching given in them, even if he should try to do so. Thus the gifts of our millionaires are an insidious poison flowing into the fountains of learning.

Mind you, this is not the claim of a prejudiced Socialist agitator. President Hadley, of Yale University, is not a Socialist agitator, but he admits the truth of this claim. He says: "Modern University teaching costs more money per capita than it ever did before, because the public wishes a university to maintain places of scientific research, and scientific research is extremely expensive. A university is more likely to obtain this money if it gives the property owners reason to believe that vested rights will not be interfered with. If we recognize vested rights in order to secure the means of progress in physical science, is there not danger that we shall stifle the spirit of independence which is equally important as a means of progress in moral science?"

Professor Bascom is not a Socialist agitator, either, but he also recognizes the danger of corrupting our university teaching in this manner. After calling attention to the "wrongful and unflinching way" in which the wealth of the Standard Oil magnate has been amassed, he asks: "Is a college at liberty to accept money gained in a manner so hostile to the public welfare? Is it at liberty, when the Government is being put to its wits' end to check this aggression, to rank itself with those who fight it?"

And the effect of riches upon the rich themselves is as bad as anything in modern life. While it is true that there are among the rich many very good citizens, it is also perfectly plain to any honest observer of conditions that great riches are producing moral havoc and disaster among the princes of wealth in this country. Mr. Carnegie has said that a man who dies rich dies disgraced, but there is even greater reason to believe that to be born rich is to be born damned. The inheritance of vast fortunes is always demoralizing.

What must the mind and soul of a woman be like who takes her toy spaniel in state to the opera to hear Caruso sing, while, in the same city, there are babies dying for lack of food? What are we to think of the dog-dinners, the monkey-dinners and the other unspeakably foolish and unspeakably vile orgies constantly reported from Newport and other places where the drones of our social system disport themselves? What shall we say of the shocking state of affairs disclosed by the disgusting reports of our "Society Scandals," except that unearned riches corrode and destroy all human virtues?

The wise King, Solomon, knew what he was talking about when he cried out: "Give me neither poverty nor riches." Unnatural poverty is bad, blighting the soul of man; and unnatural riches are likewise bad, equally blighting the soul of man. Our social system is bad for both classes, Jonathan, and a change to better and juster conditions, while it will be resisted by the rich, the drones, with all their might, will be for the common good of all. For it is well to remember that in trying to get rid of the rule of the drones, the working class is not trying to become the ruling class, to rule others as they have been ruled. We are aiming to do away with classes altogether; to make a united and free social state.

FOOTNOTES:

[3] Mark 14:7.

[4] Quar. Pub. American Statistical Association, June 1907.

VI

THE ROOT OF THE EVIL

All for ourselves and nothing for other people seems in all ages to have been the vile maxim of the masters of mankind.--Adam Smith.

Hither, ye blind, from your futile banding! Know the rights and the rights are won. Wrong shall die with the understanding, One truth clear, and the work is done.--John Boyle O'Reilly.

The great ones of the world have taken this earth of ours to themselves; they live in the midst of splendour and superfluity. The smallest nook of the land is already a possession; none may touch it or meddle with it.--Goethe.

I have by no means exhausted the evils of the system under which we live in the brief catalogue I have made for you, my friend. If it were necessary, I could compile an immense volume of authentic evidence to overwhelm you with a sense of the awful failure of our civilization to produce a free, united, healthy, happy and virtuous people, which I conceive to be the goal toward which all good and wise men should aspire. But it is dreary and unpleasant work recounting evil conditions; constantly looking at the sores of society is a morbid and soul-destroying task.

I want you now to consider the cause of industrial misery and social inequality, to ask yourself why these conditions exist. For we can never hope to remove the evils, Jonathan, until we have discovered the underlying causes. How does it happen that some people are thrifty and virtuous and yet miserably poor and that others are thriftless and sinful and yet so rich that their riches weigh them down and make them as miserable as the very poorest? Why, in the name of all that is fair and good, have we got such a stupid, wasteful, unjust and unlovely social system after all the long centuries of human experience and toil? When you can answer these questions, my friend, you will know whither to look for deliverance.

You said in your letter to me the other day, Jonathan, that you thought things were bad because of the wickedness of man's nature. Lots of people believe that. The churches have taught that doctrine for ages, but I do not believe that it is true. It is a doctrine which earnest men who have been baffled in trying to find a satisfactory explanation for the evils have accepted in desperation. It is the doctrine of pessimism, despair and wild unfaith in man. If it were true that things were so bad as they are just because men were wicked and because there never were good men enough to make them better, we should not have any ground for hope for the future.

I propose to try and show you that the wickedness of our poor human nature is not responsible for the terrible social conditions, so that you will not have to depend for your hope of a better society upon the very slender thread of the chance of getting enough good men to make conditions better. Bad conditions make bad lives, Jonathan, and will continue to do so. Instead of depending upon getting good men first to make conditions good, we must make conditions good so that good lives may flourish and grow in them naturally.

You have read a little history, I daresay, and you know that there is no truth in the old cry that "As things are now things always have been and always will be." You know that things are always changing. If George Washington could come back to earth again he would be amazed at the changes which have taken place in the United States. Going further back, Christopher Columbus would not recognize the country he discovered. And if we could go back millions of years and bring to life one of our earliest ancestors, one of the primitive cave-dwellers, and set him down in one of our great cities, the mighty houses, streets railways, telephones, telegraphs, wireless telegraphy, electric vehicles on the streets and the ships out on the river would terrify him far more than an angry tiger would. Can you think how astonished and alarmed such a primitive cave-man would be to be taken into one of your great Pittsburg mills or down into a coal mine?

No. The world has grown, Jonathan. Man has enlarged his kingdom, his power in the universe. Step by step in the evolution of the race, man has wrested from Nature her secrets. He has gone down into the deep caverns and found mineral treasuries there; he has made the angry waves of the ocean bear great, heavy burdens from shore to shore for his benefit; he has harnessed the tides and the winds that blow and caught the lightning currents, making them all his servants. Between the lowest man in the modern tenement and the cave-man there is a greater gulf than ever existed between the beast in the forest and the highest man dwelling in a cave in that far-off period.

Things are not as they are to-day because a group of clever but desperately wicked men came together and invented a scheme of society in which the many must work for the few; in which some must have more than they can use, so that they rot of excess while others have too little and rot of hunger; in which little children must toil in factories so that big strong men may loaf in clubs and dens of vice; in which some women sell themselves body and soul for bread while other women spend the sustenance of thousands upon jewels for pet dogs. No. It was no such fiendish ingenuity which devised the capitalistic system and imposed it upon mankind. It has grown up through the ages, Jonathan, and is still growing. We have grown from savagery and barbarism through various stages to our present commercial system, and the process of growth is still going on. I believe we are growing into Socialism.

There have been many forces urging mankind onward in this long evolution. Religion has played a part. Love of country has played a part. Climate and the nature of the soil have been factors. Man's ever growing curiosity, his desire to know more of the life around him, has had much to do with it. I have put the ideals of religion and patriotism first, Jonathan, because I wanted you to see that they were by no means overlooked or forgotten, but in truth they ought not to be placed first. It is the verdict of all who have made a study of social evolution that, while these factors have exerted an important influence, back of them have been the material economic conditions.

In philosophy this is the basis of a very profound theory upon which many learned volumes have been written. It is generally called "The Materialistic Conception of History," but sometimes it is called "Economic Determinism" or "The Economic Interpretation of History." The first man to set forth the theory in a very clear and connected manner was Karl Marx, upon whose teachings the Socialists of the world have placed a great deal of reliance. I don't expect you to read all the heavy and learned books written upon this subject, for many of them require that a man must be specially trained in philosophy in order to understand them. For the present I shall be quite satisfied if you will read a ten-cent pamphlet called The Communist Manifesto, by Karl Marx and Frederick Engels and, along with that, the fourth, fifth and sixth chapters of my book, Socialism, about a hundred pages altogether. These will give you a fairly clear notion of the matter. I shall not mention the hard, scientific name of this philosophy again. I don't like big words if little ones will serve.

If you enjoy reading a good story, a novel that is full of romance and adventure, I would advise you to read Before Adam, by Jack London, a Socialist writer. It is a novel, but it is also a work of science. He gives an account of the life of the first men and shows how their whole existence depended upon the crude weapons and tools, sticks picked up in the forests, which they used. They couldn't live differently than they did, because they had no other means of getting a living. How a people make their living determines how they live.

For many thousands of years, the scientists tell us, men lived in the world without owning any private property. That came into existence when men saw that one man could produce more out of the soil than he needed to eat himself. Then, when they went out to war with other tribes, the members of a tribe instead of trying to kill their enemies, made them captives and used them as slaves. They did not cease killing their foes from humane motives, because they had grown better men, but because it was more profitable.

From our point of view, slavery is a bad thing, but when it first came into existence it was a step upward and onward. If we take the history of slave societies and nations we shall soon find that their laws, their customs and their institutions were based upon the mode of producing wealth through the labor of slaves. There were two classes into which society was divided, a class of masters and a class of slaves.

When slavery broke down and gave way to feudalism there were new ways of producing wealth. The laws of feudal societies, their customs and institutions, changed to meet the needs brought about through the new methods of making things. Under slavery, the slaves made wealth for their masters and were doled out food enough to keep them alive. The slave had no rights. Under feudalism, the serfs produced wealth for the lords parts of the time, working for themselves the rest of the time. They had some rights. The bounds of freedom were widened. Under neither of these systems was there a regular system of paying wages in money, such as we have to-day. The slave gave up all his product and took what the master was pleased to give him in the way of food, clothing and shelter. The serf divided his time between producing for the owner of the soil and producing for his family. The slave produced what his owner wanted; the serf produced what either he himself or his lord wanted.

There came a time, about three hundred years ago, when the feudal system broke down before the beginnings of capitalism, the system which we are living under to-day, and which we Socialists think is breaking down as all other social systems have broken down before it. Under this system men have worked for wages and not because they wanted the things they were producing, nor because the men who employed them wanted the things, but simply because the things could be sold and a profit made in the sale.

You will remember, Jonathan, that in a former letter I dealt with the nature of wealth. We saw then that wealth in our modern society consists of an abundance of things which can be sold. At bottom, we do not make things because it is well that they should be made, because the makers need them, but simply because the capitalists see possibilities of selling the things at a profit.

I want you to consider just a moment how this works out: Here is a workingman in Springfield, Massachusetts, making deadly weapons with which other workingmen in other lands are to be killed. We go up to him as he works and inquire where the rifles are to be sent, and he very politely tells us that they are for some foreign government, say the Japanese, to be used in all probability against Russian soldiers. Suppose we ask him next what interest he has in helping the Japanese government to kill the Russian troops, how he comes to have an active hatred of the Russian soldiers. He will reply at once that he has no such feelings against the Russians; that he is not interested in having the Japanese slaughter them. Why, then, is he making the guns? He answers at once that he is only interested in getting his wages; that it is all the same to him whether he makes guns for Christians or Infidels, for Russians or Japs or Turks. His only interest is to get his wages. He would as soon be making coffins as guns, or shoes as coffins, so long as he got his wages.

Perhaps, then, the company for which he is employed has an interest in helping Japan defeat the troops of Russia. Possibly the shareholders in the company are Japanese or sympathizers with Japan. Otherwise, why should they be bothering themselves getting workpeople to make guns for Japanese soldiers to kill Russian soldiers with? So we go to the manager and ask him to explain the matter. He very politely tells us that, like the man at the bench, he has no interest in the matter at all, and that the shareholders are in the same position of being quite indifferent to the quarrel of the two nations. "Why, we are also making guns for Russia in our factory," he says, and when we ask him to explain why he tells us that "There is profit to be made and the firm cares for nothing else."

All our system revolves around that central sun of profit-making, Jonathan.

Here is a factory in which a great many people are making shoddy clothing. You can tell at a glance that it is shoddy and quite unfit for wearing. But why are the people making shoddy goods--why don't they make decent clothing, since they can do it quite as well? Why, because there is a profit for somebody in making shoddy. Here a group of men are building a house. They are making it of the poorest materials, making dingy little rooms; the building is badly constructed and it can never be other than a barracks. Why this "jerry-building?" There is no reason under the sun why poor houses should be built except that somebody hopes to make profit out of them.

Goods are adulterated and debased, even the food of the nation is poisoned, for profit. Legislatures are corrupted and courts of justice are polluted by the presence of the bribe-giver and the bribe-taker for profit. Nations are embroiled in quarrels and armies slaughter armies over questions which are, always, ultimately questions of profit. Here are children toiling in sweatshops, factories and mines while men are idle and seeking work. Why? Do we need the labor of the little ones in order to produce enough to maintain the life of the nation? No. But there are some people who are going to make a profit out of the labors which sap the strength of those little ones. Here are thousands of people hungry, clamoring for food and perishing for lack of it. They are willing to work, there are resources for them to work upon; they could easily maintain themselves in comfort and gladness if they set to work. Then why don't they set to work? Oh, Jonathan, the torment of this monotonous answer is unbearable--because no one can make a profit out of their labor they must be idle and starve, or drag out a miserable existence aided by the crumbs of cold charity!

If our social economy were such that we produced things for use, because they were useful and beautiful, we should go on producing with a good will until everybody had a plentiful supply. If we found ourselves producing too rapidly, faster than we could consume the things, we could easily slacken our pace. We could spend more time beautifying our cities and our homes, more time cultivating our minds and hearts by social intercourse and in the companionship of the great spirits of all ages, through the masterpieces of literature, music, painting and sculpture. But instead, we produce for sale and profit. When the workers have produced more than the master class can use and they themselves buy back out of their meagre wages, there is a glut in the markets of the world, unless a new market can be opened up by making war upon some defenseless, undeveloped nation.

When there is a glut in the market, Jonathan, you know what happens. Shops and factories are shut down, the number of workers employed is reduced, the army of the unemployed grows and there is a rise in the tide of poverty and misery. Yet why should it be so? Why, simply because there is a superabundance of wealth, should people be made poorer? Why should little children go without shoes just because there are loads of shoes stacked away in stores and warehouses? Why should people go without clothing simply because the warehouses are bursting with clothes? The answer is that these things must be so because we produce for profit instead of for use. All these stores of wealth belong to the class of profit-takers, the capitalist class, and they must sell and make profit.

So you see, friend Jonathan, so long as this system lasts, people must have too little because they have produced too much. So long as this system lasts, there must be periods when we say that society cannot afford to have men and women work to maintain themselves decently! But under any sane system it will surely be considered the maddest kind of folly to keep men in idleness while saying that it does not pay to keep them working. Is there any more expensive way of keeping either an ass or a man than in idleness?

The root of evil, the taproot from which the evils of modern society develop, is the profit idea. Life is subordinated to the making of profit. If it were only possible to embody that idea in human shape, what a monster ogre it would be! And how we should arraign it at the bar of human reason! Should we not call up images of the million of babes who have been needlessly and wantonly slaughtered by the Monster Idea; the images of all the maimed and wounded and killed in the wars for markets; the millions of others who have been bruised and broken in the industrial arena to secure somebody's profit, because it was too expensive to guard life and limb; the numberless victims of adulterated food and drink, of cheap tenements and shoddy clothes? Should we not call up the wretched women of our streets; the bribers and the vendors of privilege? We should surely parade in pitiable procession the dwarfed and stunted bodies of the millions born to hardship and suffering, but we could not, alas! parade the dwarfed and stunted souls, the sordid spirits for which the Monster Idea is responsible.

I ask you, Jonathan Edwards, what you really think of this "buy cheap and sell dear" idea, which is the heart and soul of our capitalistic system. Are you satisfied that it should continue?

Yet, my friend, bad as it is in its full development, and terrible as are its fruits, this idea once stood for progress. The system was a step in the liberation of man. It was an advance upon feudalism which bound the laborer to the soil. Capitalism has not been all bad; it has another, brighter side. Capitalism had to have laborers who were free to move from one place to another, even to other lands, and that need broke down the last vestiges of the old physical slavery. That was a step gained. Capitalism had to have intelligent workers and many educated ones. That put into the hands of the common people the key to the sealed treasuries of knowledge. It had to have a legal system to meet its requirements and that has resulted in the development of representative government, of something approaching political democracy; even where kings nominally rule to-day, their power is but a shadow of what it once was. Every step taken by the capitalist class for the advancement of its own interests has become in its turn a stepping-stone upon which the working-class has raised itself.

Karl Marx once said that the capitalist system provides its own gravediggers. I have cited two or three things which will illustrate his meaning. Later on, I must try and explain to you how the great "trusts" about which you complain so loudly, and which seem to be the very perfection of the capitalist ideal, lead toward Socialism at a pace which nothing can very seriously hinder, though it may be quickened by wise action on the part of the workers.

For the present I shall be satisfied, friend Jonathan, if you get it thoroughly into your mind that the source of terrible social evils, of the poverty and squalor, of the helpless misery of the great mass of the people, of most of the crime and vice and much of the disease, is the "buy cheap and sell dear" idea. The fact that we produce things for sale for the profit of a few, instead of for use and the enjoyment of all.

Get that into your mind above everything else, my friend. And try to grasp the fact, also, that the system we are now trying to change was a natural outgrowth of other conditions. It was not a wicked invention, nor was it a foolish blunder. It was a necessary and a right step in human evolution. But now it has in turn become unsuitable to the needs of the people and it must give place to something else. When a man suffers from such a disease as appendicitis, he does not talk about the "wickedness" of the vermiform appendix. He realizes, if he is a sensible man, that long ago, that was an organ which served a useful purpose in the human system. Gradually, perhaps in the course of many centuries, it has ceased to be of any use. It has lost its original functions and become a menace to the body.

Capitalism, Jonathan, is the vermiform appendix of the social organism. It has served its purpose. The profit idea has served an important function in society, but it is now useless and a menace to the body social. Our troubles are due to a kind of social appendicitis. And the remedy is to remove the useless and offending member.

VII

FROM COMPETITION TO MONOPOLY

It may be fairly said, I think, that not merely competition, but competition that was proving ruinous to many establishments, was the cause of the combinations.--Prof. J.W. Jenks.

The day of the capitalist has come, and he has made full use of it. To-morrow will be the day of the laborer, provided he has the strength and the wisdom to use his opportunities.--H. De. B. Gibbins.

Monopoly expands, ever expands, till it ends by bursting.--P.J. Proudhon.

For this is the close of an era; we have political freedom; next and right away is to come social enfranchisement.--Benjamin Kidd.

I think you realize, friend Jonathan, that the bottom principle of the present capitalist system is that there must be one class owning the land, mines, factories, railways, and other agencies of production, but not using them; and another class, using the land and other means of production, but not owning them.

Only those things are produced which there is a reasonable hope of selling at a profit. Upon no other conditions will the owners of the means of production consent to their being used. The worker who does not own the things necessary to produce wealth must work upon the terms imposed by the other fellow in most cases. The coal miner, not owning the coal mine, must agree to work for wages. So must the mechanic in the workshop and the mill-worker.

As a practical, sensible workingman, Jonathan, you know very well that if anybody says the interests of these two classes are the same it is a foolish and lying statement. You are a workingman, a wage-earner, and you know that it is to your interest to get as much wages as possible for the smallest amount of work. If you work by the day and get, let us say, two dollars for ten hours' work, it would be a great advantage to you if you could get your wages increased to three dollars and your hours of labor to eight per day, wouldn't it? And if you thought that you could get these benefits for the asking you would ask for them, wouldn't you? Of course you would, being a sensible, hard-headed American workingman.

Now, if giving these things would be quite as much to the advantage of the company as to you, the company would be just as glad to give them as you would be to receive them, wouldn't it? I am assuming, of course, that the company knows its own interests just as well as you and your fellow workmen know yours. But if you went to the officials of the company and asked them to give you a dollar more for the two hours' less work, they would not give it--unless, of course, you were strong enough to fight and compel them to accept your terms. But they would resist and you would have to fight, because your interests clashed.

That is why trade unions are formed on the one side and employers' associations upon the other. Society is divided by antagonistic interests; into exploiters and exploited.

Politicians and preachers may cry out that there are no classes in America, and they may even be foolish enough to believe it--for there are lots of very foolish politicians and preachers in the world! You may even hear a short-sighted labor leader say the same thing, but you know very well, my friend, that they are wrong. You may not be able to confute them in debate, not having their skill in wordy warfare; but your experience, your common sense, convince you that they are wrong. And all the greatest political economists are on your side. I could fill a volume with quotations from the writings of the most learned political economists of all times in support of your position, but I shall only give one quotation. It is from Adam Smith's great work, The Wealth of Nations, and I quote it partly because no better statement of the principle has ever been made by any writer, and partly also because no one can accuse Adam Smith of being a "wicked Socialist trying to set class against class." He says:

"The workmen desire to get as much, the masters to give as little as possible. The former are disposed to combine in order to raise, the latter in order to lower the wages of labor.... Masters are always and everywhere in a sort of tacit, but constant and uniform, combination, not to raise the wages of labor above their actual rate. To violate this combination is everywhere a most unpopular action, and a sort of a reproach to a master among his neighbors and equals.... Masters too sometimes enter into particular combinations to sink the wages of labor.... These are always conducted with the utmost silence and secrecy, till the moment of execution."

That is very plainly put, Jonathan. Adam Smith was a great thinker and an honest one. He was not afraid to tell the truth. I am going to quote a little further what he says about the combinations of workingmen to increase their wages:

"Such combinations, [i.e., to lower wages] however, are frequently resisted by a contrary defensive combination of the workmen; who sometimes too, without any provocation of this kind, combine of their own accord to raise the price of labor. Their usual pretenses are, sometimes the high price of provisions; sometimes the great profit which their masters make by their work. But whether these combinations be offensive or defensive, they are always abundantly heard of. In order to bring the point to a speedy decision, they have always recourse to the loudest clamour, and sometimes to the most shocking violence and outrage. They are desperate, and act with the extravagance and folly of desperate men, who must either starve, or frighten their masters into an immediate compliance with their demands. The masters upon these occasions are just as clamorous upon the other side, and never cease to call aloud for the assistance of the civil magistrate, and the rigorous execution of those laws which have been enacted with so much severity against the combinations of servants, laborers, and journeymen.

"But though in disputes with their workmen, masters must generally have the advantage, there is however a certain rate, below which it seems impossible to reduce, for any considerable time, the ordinary wages even of the lowest species of labor.

"A man must always live by his work, and his wages must at least be sufficient to maintain him. They must even upon most occasions be somewhat more; otherwise it would be impossible for him to bring up a family, and the race of such workmen could not last beyond the first generation."

Now, my friend, I know that some of your pretended friends, especially politicians, will tell you that Adam Smith wrote at the time of the American Revolution; that his words applied to England in that day, but not to the United States to-day. I want you to be honest with yourself, to consider candidly whether in your experience as a workman you have found conditions to be, on the whole, just as Adam Smith's words describe them. I trust your own good sense in this and everything. Don't let the politicians frighten you with a show of book learning: do your own thinking.

Capitalism began when a class of property owners employed other men to work for wages. The tendency was for wages to keep at a level just sufficient to enable the workers to maintain themselves and families. They had to get enough for families, you see, in order to reproduce their kind--to keep up the supply of laborers.

Competition was the law of life in the first period of capitalism. Capitalists competed with each other for markets. They were engaged in a mad scramble for profits. Foreign countries were attacked and new markets opened up; new inventions were rapidly introduced. And while the workers found that in normal conditions the employers were in what Adam Smith calls "a tacit combination" to keep wages down to the lowest level, and were obliged to combine into unions, there were times when, owing to the fierce competition among the employers, and the demand for labor being greatly in excess of the supply, wages went up without a struggle owing to the fact that one employer would try to outbid another. In other words, temporarily, the natural, "tacit combination" of the employers, to keep down wages, sometimes broke down.

Competition was called "the life of trade" in those days, and in a sense it was so. Under its mighty urge, new continents were explored and developed and brought within the circle of civilization. Sometimes this was done by means of brutal and bloody wars, for capitalism is never particular about the methods it adopts. To get profits is its only concern, and though its shekels "sweat blood and dirt," to adapt a celebrated phrase of Karl Marx, nobody cares. Under stress of competition, also, the development of mechanical production went on at a terrific pace; navigation was developed, so that the ocean became as a common highway.

In short, Jonathan, it is no wonder that men sang the praises of competition, that some of the greatest thinkers of the time looked upon competition as something sacred. Even the workers, seeing that they got higher wages when the keen and fierce competition created an excessive demand for labor, joined in the adoration of competition as a principle--but among themselves, in their struggles for better conditions, they avoided competition as much as possible and combined. Their instincts as wage-earners made them keen to see the folly of division and competition among themselves.

So competition, considered in connection with the evolution of society, had many good features. The competitive period was just as "good" as any other period in history and no more "wicked" than any other period.

But there was another side to the shield. As the competitive struggle among individual capitalists went on the weakest were crushed to the wall and fell down into the ranks of the wage workers. There was no system in production. Word came to the commercial world that there was a great market for certain manufactures in a foreign land and at once hundreds and even thousands of factories were worked to their utmost limit to meet that demand. The result was that in a little while the thing was overdone: there was a glut in the market, often attended by panic, stagnation and disaster. Rathbone Greg summed up the evils of competition in the following words:

"Competition gluts our markets, enables the rich to take advantage of the necessity of the poor, makes each man snatch the bread out of his neighbor's mouth, converts a nation of brethren into a mass of hostile units, and finally involves capitalists and laborers in one common ruin."

The crises due to this unregulated production, and the costliness of the struggles, led to the formation of joint-stock companies. Competition was giving way before a stronger force, the force of co-operation. There was still competition, but it was more and more between giants. To adopt a very homely simile, the bigger fish ate up the little ones so long as there were any, and then turned to a struggle among themselves.

Another thing that forced the development of industry and commerce away from competitive methods was the increasing costliness of the machinery of production. The new inventions, first of steam-power and later of electricity, involved an immense outlay, so that many persons had to combine their capitals in one common fund.

This process of eliminating competition has gone on with remarkable swiftness, so that we have now the great Trust Problem. Everyone recognizes to-day that the trusts practically control the life of the nation. It is the supreme issue in our politics and a challenge to the heart and brain of the nation.

Fifty years ago Karl Marx, the great Socialist economist, made the remarkable prophecy that this condition would arise. He lived in the heyday of competition, when it seemed utter folly to talk about the end of competition. He analyzed the situation, pointed to the process of big capitalists crushing out the little capitalists, the union of big capitalists, and the inevitable drift toward monopoly. He predicted that the process would continue until the whole industry, the main agencies of production and distribution at any rate, would be centralized in a few great monopolies, controlled by a very small handful of men. He showed with wonderful clearness that capitalism, the Great Idea of buy cheap and sell dear, carried within itself the germs of its own destruction.

And, of course, the wiseacres laughed. The learned ignorance of the wiseacre always compels him to laugh at the man with an idea that is new.

Didn't the wiseacres imprison Galileo? Haven't they persecuted the pioneers in all ages? But Time has a habit of vindicating the pioneers while consigning the scoffing wiseacres to oblivion. Fifty years is a short time in human evolution but it has sufficed to establish the right of Marx to an honored place among the pioneers.

More than twenty-five years after Marx made his great prediction, there came to this country on a visit Mr. H.M. Hyndman, an English economist who is also known as one of the foremost living exponents of Socialism. The intensity of the competitive struggle was most marked, but he looked below the surface and saw a subtle current, a drift toward monopoly, which had gone unnoticed. He predicted the coming of the era of great trusts and combines. Again the wiseacres in their learned ignorance laughed and derided. The amiable gentleman who plays the part of flunkey at the Court of St. James, in London, wearing plush knee breeches, silver-buckled shoes and powdered wig, a marionette in the tinseled show of King Edward's court, was one of the wiseacres. He was then editor of the New York Tribune, and he declared that Mr. Hyndman was a "fool traveler" for making such a prediction. But in the very next year the Standard Oil Company was formed!

So we have the trust problem with us. Out of the bitter competitive struggle there has come a new condition, a new form of industrial ownership and enterprise. From the cradle to the grave we are encompassed by the trust.

Now, friend Jonathan, I need not tell you that the trusts have got the nation by the throat. You know it. But there is a passage, a question, in the letter you wrote me the other day from which I gather that you have not given the matter very close attention. You ask "How will the Socialists destroy the trusts which are hurting the people?"

I suppose that comes from your old associations with the Democratic Party. You think that it is possible to destroy the trusts, to undo the chain of social evolution, to go back twenty or fifty years to competitive conditions. You would restore competition. I have purposely gone into the historical development of the trust in order to show you how useless it would be to destroy the trusts and introduce competition again, even if that were possible. Now that you have mentally traced the origin of monopoly to its causes in competition, don't you see that if we could destroy the monopoly to-morrow and start fresh upon a basis of competition, the process of "big fish eat little fish" would begin again at once--for that is competition? And if the big ones eat the little ones up, then fight among themselves, won't the result be as before--that either one will crush the other, leaving a monopoly, or the competitors will join hands and agree not to fight, leaving monopoly again?

And, Jonathan, if there should be a return to the old-fashioned, free-for-all scramble for markets, would it be any better for the workers? Would there not be the same old struggle between the capitalists and the workers? Would not the workers still have to give much for little; to wear their lives away grinding out profits for the masters of their bread, of their very lives? Would there not be gluts as before, with panics, misery, unemployed armies sullenly parading the streets; idlers in mansions and toilers in hovels? You know very well that there would be all these, my friend, and I know that you are too sensible a fellow to think any longer about destroying the trusts. It cannot be done, Jonathan, and it would not be a good thing if it could be done.

I think, my friend, that you will see upon reflection that there are many excellent features about the trust which it would be criminal and foolish to destroy had we the power. Competition means waste, foolish and unnecessary waste. Trusts have been organized expressly to do away with the waste of men and natural resources. They represent economical production. When Mr. Perkins, of the New York Life Insurance Company, was testifying before the insurance investigating committee he gave expression to the philosophy of the trust movement by saying that, in the modern view, competition is the law of death and that co-operation and organization represent life and progress.

While the wage-workers are probably in many respects better off as a result of the trustification of industry, it would be idle to deny that there are many evils connected with it. No one who views the situation calmly can deny that the trusts exert an enormous power over the government of the country, that they are, in fact, the real government of the country, exercising far more control over the lives of the common people than the regularly constituted, constitutional government of the country does. It is also true that they can arbitrarily fix prices in many instances, so that the natural law of value is set aside and the workers are exploited as consumers, as purchasers of the things necessary to life, just as they are exploited as producers.

Of course, friend Jonathan, wages must meet the cost of living. If prices rise considerably, wages must sooner or later follow, and if prices fall wages likewise will fall sooner or later. But it is important to remember that when prices fall wages are quick to follow, while when prices soar higher and higher wages are very slow to follow. That is why it wouldn't do us any good to have a law regulating prices, supposing that a law forcing down prices could be enacted and enforced. Wages would follow prices downward with wonderful swiftness. And that is why, also, we do need to become the masters of the wealth we produce. For wages climb upward with leaden feet, my friend, when prices soar with eagle wings. It is always the workers who are at a disadvantage in a system where one class controls the means of producing and distributing wealth.

But, friend Jonathan, that is due to the fact that the advantages of the trust form of industry are not used as well as they might be. They are all grasped by the master class. The trouble with the trust is simply this: the people as a whole do not share the benefits. We continue the same old wage system under the new forms of industry: we have not changed our mode of distributing the wealth produced so as to conform to the new modes of producing it. The heart of the economic conflict is right there.

We must find a remedy for this, Jonathan. Labor unionism is a good thing, but it is no remedy for this condition. It is a valuable weapon with, which to fight for better wages and shorter hours, and every workingman ought to belong to the union of his trade or calling. But unionism does not and cannot do away with the profit system; it cannot break the power of the trusts to extort monopoly prices from the people. To do these things we must bring into play the forces of government: we must vote a new status for the trust. The union is for the economic struggle of groups of workers day by day against the master class so long as the present class division exists. But that is not a solution of the problem. What we need to do is to vote the class divisions out of existence. We need to own the trusts, Jonathan!

This is the Socialist position. What is needed now is the harmonizing of our social relations with the new forms of production. When private property came into the primitive world in the form of slavery, social relations were changed and from a rude communism society passed into a system of individualism and class rule. When, later on, slave labor gave way before serf labor, the social relations were again modified to correspond. When capitalism came, with wage-paid labor as its basis, all the laws and institutions which stood in the way of the free development of the new principle were swept away; new social relations were established, new laws and institutions introduced to meet its needs.

To-day, in America, we are suffering because our social relations are not in harmony with the changed methods of producing wealth. We have got the laws and institutions which were designed to meet the needs of competitive industry. They suited those old conditions fairly well, but they do not suit the new.

In a former letter, you will remember, I likened our present suffering to a case of appendicitis, that society suffers from the trouble set up within by an organ which has lost its function and needs to be cut out. Perhaps I might better liken society to a woman in the travail of childbirth, suffering the pangs of labor incidental to the deliverance of the new life within her womb. The trust marks the highest development of capitalist society: it can go no further.

The Old Order changeth, yielding place to new.

And the new order, waiting now for deliverance from the womb of the old, is Socialism, the fraternal state. Whether the birth of the new order is to be peaceful or violent and painful, whether it will be ushered in with glad shouts of triumphant men and women, or with the noise of civil strife, depends, my good friend, upon the manner in which you and all other workers discharge your responsibilities as citizens. That is why I am so anxious to set the claims of Socialism clearly before you: I want you to work for the peaceful revolution of society, Jonathan.

For the present, I am only going to ask you to read a little five cent pamphlet, by Gaylord Wilshire, called The Significance of the Trust, and a little book by Frederick Engels, called Socialism, Utopian and Scientific. Later on, when I have had a chance to explain Socialism in a general way, and must then leave you to your own resources, I intend to make for you a list of books, which I hope you will be able to read.

You see, Jonathan, I remember always that you wrote me: "Whether Socialism is good or bad, wise or foolish, I want to know." The best way to know is to study the question for yourself.

VIII

WHAT SOCIALISM IS AND WHAT IT IS NOT

Socialism is industrial democracy. It would put an end to the irresponsible control of economic interests, and substitute popular self-government in the industrial as in the political world.--Charles H. Vail.

Socialism says that man, machinery and land must be brought together; that the toll gates of capitalism must be torn down, and that every human being's opportunity to produce the means with which to sustain life shall be considered as sacred as his right to live.--Allan L. Benson.

Socialism means that all those things upon which the people in common depend shall by the people in common be owned and administered. It means that the tools of employment shall belong to their creators and users; that all production shall be for the direct use of the producers; that the making of goods for profit shall come to an end; that we shall all be workers together; and that all opportunities shall be open and equal to all men.--National Platform of the Socialist Party, 1904.

Socialism does not consist in violently seizing upon the property of the rich and sharing it out amongst the poor.

Socialism is not a wild dream of a happy land where the apples will drop off the trees into our open mouths, the fish come out of the rivers and fry themselves for dinner, and the looms turn out ready-made suits of velvet with golden buttons without the trouble of coaling the engine. Neither is it a dream of a nation of stained-glass angels, who never say damn, who always love their neighbors better than themselves, and who never need to work unless they wish to.--Robert Blatchford.

By this time, friend Jonathan, you have, I hope, got rid of the notion that Socialism is a ready-made scheme of society which a few wise men have planned, and which their followers are trying to get adopted. I have spent some time and effort trying to make it perfectly plain to you that great social changes are not brought about in that fashion.

Socialism then, is a philosophy of human progress, a theory of social evolution, the main outlines of which I have already sketched for you. Because the subject is treated at much greater length in some of the books I have asked you to read, it is not necessary for me to elaborate the theory. It will be sufficient, probably, for me to restate, in a very few words, the main principles of that theory:

The present social system throughout the civilized world is not the result of deliberately copying some plan devised by wise men. It is the result of long centuries of growth and development. From our present position we look back over the blood-blotted pages of history, back to the ages before men began to write their history and their thoughts, through the centuries of which there is only faint tradition; we go even further back, to the very beginning of human existence, to the men-apes and the ape-men whose existence science has made clear to us, and we see the race engaged in a long struggle to

Move upward, working out the beast And let the ape and tiger die.

We look for the means whereby the progress of man has been made, and find that his tools have been, so to say, the ladder upon which he has risen in the age-long climb from bondage toward brotherhood, from being a brute armed with a club to the sovereign of the universe, controlling tides, harnessing winds, gathering the lightning in his hands and reaching to the farthest star.

We find in every epoch of that long evolution the means of producing wealth as the center of all, transforming government, laws, institutions and moral codes to meet their limitations and their needs. Nothing has ever been strong enough to restrain the economic forces in social evolution. When laws and customs have stood in the way of the economic forces they have been burst asunder as by some mighty leaven, or hurled aside in the cyclonic sweep of revolutions.

Have you ever gone into the country, Jonathan, and noticed an immense rock split and shattered by the roots of a tree, or perhaps by the might of an insignificant looking fungus? I have, many times, and I never see such a rock without thinking of its aptness as an illustration of this Socialist philosophy. A tiny acorn tossed by the wind finds lodgment in some small crevice of a rock which has stood for thousands of years, a rock so big and strong that men choose it as an emblem of the Everlasting. Soon the warm caresses of the sun and the rain wake the latent life in the acorn; the shell breaks and a frail little shoot of vegetable life appears, so small that an infant could crush it. Yet that weak and puny thing grows on unobserved, striking its rootlets farther into the crevice of the rock. And when there is no more room for it to grow, it does not die, but makes room for itself by shattering the rock.

Economic forces are like that, my friend, they must expand and grow. Nothing can long restrain them. A new method of producing wealth broke up the primitive communism of prehistoric man; another change in the methods of production hurled the feudal barons from power and forced the establishment of a new social system. And now, we are on the eve of another great change--nay, we are in the very midst of the change. Capitalism is doomed! Not because men think it is wicked, but because the development of the great industrial trusts compels a new political and social system to meet the needs of the new mode of production.

Something has got to give way to the irresistible growing force! A change is inevitable. And the change must be to Socialism. That is the belief of the Socialists, Jonathan, which I am trying to make you understand. Mind, I do not say that the coming change will be the last change in human evolution, that there will be no further development after Socialism. I do not know what lies beyond, nor to what heights humanity may attain in future years. It may be that thousands or millions of years from now the race will have attained to such a state of growth and power that the poorest and weakest man then alive will be so much superior to the greatest men alive to-day, our best scholars, poets, artists, inventors and statesmen, as these are superior to the cave-man. It may be. I do not know. Only a fool would seek to set mete and bound to man's possibilities.

We are concerned only with the change that is imminent, the change that is now going on before our eyes. We say that the outcome of society's struggle with the trust problem must be the control of the trust by society. That the outcome of the struggle between the master class and the slave class, between the wealth makers and the wealth takers, must be the victory of the makers.

Throughout all history, ever since the first appearance of private property--

of slavery and land ownership--there have been class struggles. Slave and slave-owner, serf and baron, wage-slave and capitalist--so the classes have struggled. And what has been the issue, thus far? Chattel slavery gave way to serfdom, in which the oppression was lighter and the oppressed gained some measure of human recognition. Serfdom, in its turn, gave way to the wages system, in which, despite many evils, the oppressed class lives upon a far higher plane than the slave and serf classes from whence it sprang. Now, with the capitalists unable to hold and manage the great machinery of production which has been developed, with the workers awakened to their power, armed with knowledge, with education, and, above all, with the power to make the laws, the government, what they will, can anybody doubt what the outcome will be?

It is impossible to believe that we shall continue to leave the things upon which all depend in the hands of a few members of society. Now that production has been so organized that it can be readily controlled and directed from a few centers, it is possible for the first time in the history of civilization for men to live together in peace and plenty, owning in common the things which must be used in common, which are needed in common; leaving to private ownership the things which can be privately owned without injury to society. And that is Socialism.

I have explained the philosophy of social evolution upon which modern Socialism is based as clearly as I could do in the space at my disposal. I want you to think it out for yourself, Jonathan. I want you to get the enthusiasm and the inspiration which come from a realization of the fact that progress is the law of Nature; that mankind is ever marching upward and onward; that Socialism is the certain inheritor of all the ages of struggle, suffering and accumulation.

And above all, I want you to realize the position of your class, my friend, and your duty to stand with your class, not only as a union man, but as a voter and a citizen.

As a system of political economy I need say little of Socialism, beyond recounting some of the things we have already considered. A great many learned ignorant men, like Mr. Mallock, for instance, are fond of telling the workers that the economic teachings of Socialism are unsound; that Karl Marx was really a very superficial thinker whose ideas have been entirely discredited.

Now, Karl Marx has been dead twenty-five years, Jonathan. His great work was done a generation ago. Being just a human being, like the rest of us, it is not to be supposed that he was infallible. There are some things in his writings which cannot be accepted without modification. But what does that matter, so long as the essential principles are sound and true? When we think of a great man like Lincoln we do not trouble about the little things--the trivial mistakes he made; we consider only the big things, the noble things, the true things, he said and did.

But there are lots of little-minded, little-souled people in the world who have eyes only for the little flaws and none at all for the big, strong and enduring things in a man's work. I never think of these critics of Marx without calling to mind an incident I witnessed two or three years ago at an art exhibition in New York. There was placed on exhibition a famous Greek marble, a statue of Aphrodite. Many people went to see it and on several occasions when I saw it I observed that some people had been enough stirred to place little bunches of flowers at the feet of the statue as a tender tribute to its beauty. But one day I was greatly annoyed by the presence of a critical woman who had discovered a little flaw in the statue, where a bit had been broken off. She chattered about it like an excited magpie. Poor soul, she had no eyes for the beauty of the thing, the mystery which shrouded its past stirred no emotions in her breast. She was only just big enough in mind and soul to see the flaw. I pitied her, Jonathan, as I pity many of the critics who write learned books to prove that the economic principles of Socialism are wrong. I cannot read such a book but a vision rises before my mind's eye of that woman and the statue.

I believe that the great fundamental principles laid down by Karl Marx cannot be refuted, because they are true. But it is just as well to bear in mind that Socialism does not depend upon Karl Marx. If all his works could be destroyed and his name forgotten there would still be a Socialist movement to contend with. The question is: Are the economic principles of Socialism as it is taught to-day true or false?

The first principle is that wealth in modern society consists in an abundance of things which can be sold for profit.

So far as I know, there is no economist of note who makes any objection to that statement. I know that sometimes political economists confuse their readers and themselves by a loose use of the term wealth, including in it many things which have nothing at all to do with economics. Good health and cheerful spirits, for example, are often spoken of as wealth and there is a certain primal sense in which that word is rightly applied to them. You remember the poem by Charles Mackay--

Cleon hath a million acres, ne'er a one have I; Cleon dwelleth in a palace, in a cottage I; Cleon hath a dozen fortunes, not a penny I; Yet the poorer of the twain is Cleon, and not I.

In a great moral sense that is all true, Jonathan, but from the point of view of political economy, Cleon of the million acres, the palace and the dozen fortunes must be regarded as the richer of the two.

The second principle is that wealth is produced by labor applied to natural resources.

The only objections to this, the only attempts ever made to deny its truth, have been based upon a misunderstanding of the meaning of the word "labor." If a man came to you in the mill one day, and said: "See that great machine with all its levers and springs and wheels working in such beautiful harmony. It was made entirely by manual workers, such as moulders, blacksmiths and machinists; no brain workers had anything to do with it," you would suspect that man of being a fool, Jonathan. You know, even though you are no economist, that the labor of the inventor and of the men who drew the plans of the various parts was just as necessary as the labor of the manual workers. I have already shown you, when discussing the case of Mr. Mallock, that Socialists have never claimed that wealth was produced by manual labor alone, and that brain labor is always unproductive. All the great political economists have included both mental and manual labor in their use of the term, that being, indeed, the only sensible use of the word known to our language.

It is very easy work, my friend, for a clever juggler of words to erect a straw man, label the dummy "Socialism" and then pull it to pieces. But it is not very useful work, nor is it an honest intellectual occupation. I say to you, friend Jonathan, that when writers like Mr. Mallock contend that "ability," as distinguished from labor, must be considered as a principal factor in production, they must be regarded as being either mentally weak or deliberate perverters of the truth. You know, and every man of fair sense knows, that ability in the abstract never could produce anything at all.

Take Mr. Edison, for example. He is a man of wonderful ability--one of the greatest men of this or any other age. Suppose Mr. Edison were to say: "I know I have a great deal of ability; I think that I will just sit down with folded hands and depend upon the mere possession of my ability to make a living for me"--what do you think would happen? If Mr. Edison were to go to some lonely spot, without tools or food, making up his mind that he need not work; that he could safely depend upon his ability to produce food for him while he sat idle or slept, he would starve. Ability is like a machine, Jonathan. If you have the finest machine in the world and keep it in a garret it will produce nothing at all. You might as well have a pile of stones there as the machine.

But connect the machine with the motor and place a competent man in charge of it, and the machine at once becomes a means of production. Ability is likewise useless and impotent unless it is expressed in the form of either manual or mental labor. And when it is so embodied in labor, it is quite useless and foolish to talk of ability as separate from the labor in which it is embodied.

The third principle of Socialist economics is that the value of things produced for sale is, under normal conditions, determined by the amount of labor socially necessary, on an average, for their production. This is called the labor theory of value.

Many people have attacked this theory, Jonathan, and it has been "refuted," "upset," "smashed" and "destroyed" by nearly every hack writer on economics living. But, for some reason, the number of people who accept it is constantly increasing in spite of the number of times it has been "exposed" and "refuted." It is worth our while to consider it briefly.

You will observe that I have made two important qualifications in the above statement of the theory: first, that the law applies only to things produced for sale, and second, that it is only under normal conditions that it holds true. Many very clever men try to prove this law of value wrong by citing the fact that articles are sometimes sold for enormous prices, out of all proportion to the amount of labor it took to produce them in the first instance. For example, it took Shakespeare only a few minutes to write a letter, we may suppose, but if a genuine letter in the poet's handwriting were offered for sale in one of the auction rooms where such things are sold it would fetch an enormous price; perhaps more than the yearly salary of the President of the United States.

The value of the letter would not be due to the amount of labor Shakespeare devoted to the writing of it, but to its rarity. It would have what the economists call a "scarcity value." The same is true of a great many other things, such as historical relics, great works of art, and so on. These things are in a class by themselves. But they constitute no important part of the business of modern society. We are not concerned with them, but with the ordinary, every day production of goods for sale. The truth of this law of value is not to be determined by considering these special objects of rarity, but the great mass of things produced in our workshops and factories.

Now, note the second qualification. I say that the value of things produced for sale under normal conditions is determined by the amount of labor socially necessary, on an average, for their production. Some of the clever, learnedly-ignorant writers on Socialism think that they have completely destroyed this theory of value when they have only misrepresented it and crushed the image of their own creating.

It does not mean that if a quick, efficient workman, with good tools, takes a day to make a coat, while another workman, who is slow, clumsy and inefficient, and has only poor tools, takes six days to make a table that the table will be worth six coats upon the market. That would be a foolish proposition, Jonathan. It would mean that if one workman made a coat in one day, while another workman took two days to make exactly the same kind of coat, that the one made by the slow, inefficient workman would bring twice as much as the other, even though they were so much alike that they could not be distinguished one from the other.

Only an ignoramus could believe that. No Socialist writer ever made such a foolish claim, yet all the attacks upon the economic principles of Socialism are based upon that idea!

Now that I have told you what it does not mean, let me try to make plain just what it does mean. I shall use a very simple illustration which you can readily apply to the whole of industry for yourself. If it ordinarily takes a day to make a coat, if that is the average time taken, and it also takes on an average a day to make a table, then, also on an average, one coat will be worth just as much as one table. But I must explain that it is not possible to bring the production of coats and tables down to the simple measurement. When the tailor takes the piece of cloth to cut out the coat, he has in that material something that already embodies human labor. Somebody had to weave that cloth upon a loom. Before that somebody had to make the loom.

And before that loom could make cloth somebody had to raise sheep and shear them to get the wool. And before the carpenter could make the table, somebody had to go into the forest and fell a tree, after which somebody had to bring that tree, cut up into planks or logs, to the carpenter. And before he could use the lumber somebody had to make the tools with which he worked.

I think you will understand now why I placed emphasis on the words "socially necessary." It is not possible for the individual buyer to ascertain just how much social labor is contained in a coat or a table, but their values are fixed by the competition and higgling which is the law of capitalism. "It jest works out so," as an old negro preacher said to me once.

I have said that competition is the law of capitalism. All political economists recognize that as true. But we have, as I have explained in a former letter, come to a point where capitalism has broken away from competition in many industries. We have a state of affairs under which the economic laws of competitive society do not apply. Monopoly prices have always been regarded as exceptions to economic law.

If this technical economic discussion seems a little bit difficult, I beg you nevertheless to try and master it, Jonathan. It will do you good to think out these questions. Perhaps I can explain more clearly what is meant by monopoly conditions being exceptional. All through the Middle Ages it was the custom for governments to grant monopolies to favored subjects, or to sell them in order to raise ready money. Queen Elizabeth, for instance, granted and sold many such monopolies.

A man who had a monopoly of something which nearly everybody had to use could fix his own price, the only limit being the people's patience or their ability to pay. The same thing is true of patented articles and of monopolies granted to public service corporations. Generally, it is true, in the franchises of these corporations, nowadays, there is a price limit fixed beyond which they must not go, but it is still true that the normal competitive economic law has been set aside by the creation of monopoly.

When a trust is formed, or when there is a price agreement, or what is politely called "an understanding among gentlemen" to that effect, a similar thing happens. We have monopoly prices.

This is an important thing for the working class, though it is sometimes forgotten. How much your wages will secure in the way of necessities is just as important to you as the amount of wages you get. In other words, the amount you can get in comforts and commodities for use is just as important as the amount you can get in dollars and cents. Sometimes money wages increase while real wages decrease. I could fill a book with statistics to show this, but I will only quote one example. Professor Rauschenbusch cites it in his excellent book, Christianity and the Social Crisis, a book I should like you to read, Jonathan. He quotes Dun's Review, a standard financial authority, to the effect that what $724 would buy in 1897 it took $1013 to buy in 1901.

I know that I could make your wife see the importance of this, my friend. She would tell you that when from time to time you have announced that your wages were to be increased five or ten per cent. she has made plans for spending the money upon little home improvements, or perhaps for laying it aside for the dreaded "rainy day." Perhaps she thought of getting a new rug, or a new sideboard for the dining-room; or perhaps it was a piano for your daughter, who is musical, she had set her heart on getting. The ten per cent. increase seemed to make it all so easy and certain! But after a little while she found that somehow the ten per cent. did not bring the coveted things; that, although she was just as careful as could be, she couldn't save, nor get the things she hoped to get.

Often you and I have heard the cry of trouble: "I don't know how or why it is, but though I get ten per cent. more wages I am no better off than before."

The Socialist theory of value is all right, my friend, and has not been disturbed by the assaults made upon it by a host of little critics. But Socialists have always known that the laws of competitive society do not apply to monopoly, and that the monopolist has an increased power to exploit and oppress the worker. That is one of the chief reasons why we demand that the great monopolies be transformed into common, or social, property.

The fourth principle of Socialist economics is that the wages of the workers represent only a part of the value of their labor product. The remainder is divided among the non-producers in rent, interest and profit. The fortunes of the rich idlers come from the unpaid-for labor of the working class. This is the great theory of "surplus value," which economists are so fond of attacking.

I am not going to say much about the controversy concerning this theory, Jonathan. In the first place, you are not an economist, and there is a great deal in the discussion which is wholly irrelevant and unprofitable; and, in the second place, you can study the question for yourself. There are excellent chapters upon the subject in Vail's Principles of Scientific Socialism, Boudin's The Theoretical System of Karl Marx, and Hyndman's Economics of Socialism. You will also find a simple exposition of the subject in my Socialism, A Summary and Interpretation of Socialist Principles. It will also be well to read Wage-Labor and Capital, a five cent booklet by Karl Marx.

But you do not need to be an economist to understand the essential principles of this theory of surplus value and to judge of its truth. I have never flattered you, Jonathan, as you know; I am in earnest when I say that I am content to leave the matter to your own judgment. I attach more importance to your decision, based upon a plain, matter-of-fact observation of actual life, than to the opinion of many a very learned economist cloistered away from the real world in a musty atmosphere of books and mental abstractions. So think it out for yourself, my friend.

You know that when a man takes a job as a wage-worker, he enters into a contract to give something in return for a certain amount of money. What is it that he thus sells? Not his actual labor, but his power and will to labor. In other words, he undertakes to exert himself in a manner desired by the capitalist who employs him for so much an hour, so much a day, or so much a week as the case may be.

Now, how are the wages fixed? What determines the amount a man gets for his labor? There are several factors. Let us consider them one by one:

First, the man must have enough to keep himself alive and able to work. If he does not get that much he will die, or be unfit to work. Second, in order that the race may be maintained, and that there may be a constant supply of labor, it is necessary that men as a rule should have families. So, as we saw in a quotation from Adam Smith in an earlier letter, the wages must, on an average, be enough to keep, not only the man himself but those dependent upon him. These are the bottom requirements of wages.

Now, the tendency is for wages to keep somewhere near this bottom level. If nothing else interfered they would always tend to that level. First of all, there is no scientific organization of the labor force of the world. Sometimes the demand for labor in a particular trade exceeds the supply, and then wages rise. Sometimes the supply is greater than the demand, and then wages drop toward the bottom level. If the man looking for a job is so fortunate as to know that there are many places open to him, he will not accept low wages; on the other hand, if the employer knows that there are ten men for every job, he will not pay high wages. So, as with the prices of things in general, supply and demand enter into the question of the price of labor in any given time or place.

Then, also, by combination workingmen can sometimes raise their wages. They can bring about a sort of monopoly-price for their labor-power. It is not an absolute monopoly-price, however, for the reason that, almost invariably, there are men outside of the unions, whose competition has to be withstood. Also, the means of production and the accumulated surplus belong to the capitalists so that they can generally starve the workers into submission, or at least compromise, in any struggle aiming at the establishment of monopoly-prices for labor-power.

But there is one thing the workers can never do, except by destroying capitalism: they cannot get wages equal to the full value of their product. That would destroy the capitalist system, which is based upon profit-making. All the luxury and wealth of the non-producers is wrung from the labor of the producers. You can see that for yourself, Jonathan, and I need not argue it further.

I do not care very much whether you call the part of the wealth which goes to the non-producers "surplus value," or whether you call it something else. The name is not of great importance to us. We care only for the reality. But I do want you to get firm hold of the simple fact that when an idler gets a dollar he has not earned, some worker must get a dollar less than he has earned.

Don't be buncoed by the word-jugglers who tell you that the profits of the capitalists are the "fruits of abstinence," or the "reward of managing ability," sometimes also called the "wages of superintendence."

These and other attempted explanations of capitalists' profits are simply old wives' fables, Jonathan. Let us look for a minute at the first of these absurd attempts to explain away the fact that profit is only another name for unpaid-for labor. You know very well that abstinence never yet produced anything. If I have a dollar in my pocket and I say to myself, "I will not spend this dollar: I will abstain from using it," the dollar does not increase in any way. It remains just a dollar and no more. If I have a loaf of bread or a bottle of wine and say to myself, "I will not use this bread, or this wine, but will keep it in the cupboard," you know very well that I shall not get any increase as a result of my abstinence. I do not get anything more than I actually save.

Now, I am perfectly willing that any man shall have all that he can save out of his own earnings. If no man had more there would be no need of talking about "legislation to limit fortunes," no need of protest against "swollen fortunes."

But now suppose, friend Jonathan, that while I have the dollar, representing my "abstinence," in my pocket, a man who has not a dollar comes to me and says, "I really must have a dollar to get food for my wife and baby, or they will die. Lend me a dollar until next week and I will pay you back two dollars." If I lend him the dollar and next week take his two dollars, that is what is called the reward of my abstinence. But in truth it is something quite different. It is usury. Just because I happen to have something the other fellow has not got, and which he must have, he is compelled to pay me interest. If he also had a dollar in his pocket, I could get no interest from him.

It would be just the same if I had not abstained from anything. If, for example, I had found the dollar which some other careful fellow had lost, I could still get interest upon it. Or if I had inherited money from my father, it might happen that, so far from being abstemious and thrifty, I had been most extravagant, while the fellow who came to borrow had been very thrifty and abstemious, but still unable to provide for his family. Yet I should make him pay me interest.

As a matter of fact, my friend, the rich have not abstained from anything. They have not accumulated riches out of their savings, through abstaining from buying things. On the contrary, they have bought and enjoyed the costliest things. They have lived in fine houses, worn costly clothing, eaten the choicest food, sent their sons and daughters to the most expensive schools and colleges.

From all of these things the workers have abstained, Jonathan. They have abstained from living in fine houses and lived in poor houses; they have abstained from wearing costly clothes and worn the cheapest and poorest clothes; they have abstained from choice food and eaten only food that is coarse and cheap; they have abstained from sending their sons and daughters to expensive schools and colleges and sent them only to the lower grades of the public schools. If abstinence were a source of wealth, the working people of every country would be rich, for they have abstained from nearly everything that is worth while.

There is one thing the rich have abstained from, however, which the poor have indulged in freely--and that is work. I never heard of a man getting rich through his own labor.

Even the inventor does not get rich by means of his own labor. To begin with, there is no invention which is purely an individual undertaking. I was talking the other day with one of the world's great inventors upon this subject. He was explaining to me how he came to invent a certain machine which has made his name famous. He explained that for many years men had been facing a great difficulty and other inventors had been trying to devise some means of meeting it. He had, therefore, to begin with, the experience of thousands of men during many years to give him a clear idea of what was required. And that was a great thing to start with, Jonathan.

Secondly, he had the experiments of all the numerous other inventors to guide him: he could profit by their failures. Not only did he know what to avoid, because that great fund of others' experience, but he also got many useful ideas from the work of some of the men who were on the right line without knowing it. "I could not have invented it if it were not for the men who went before me," he said.

Another point, Jonathan: In the wonderful machine the inventor was discussing there are wheels and levers and springs. Somebody had to invent the wheel, the lever and the spring before there could be a machine at all. Who was it, I wonder! Do you know who made the first wheel, or the first lever? Of course you don't! Nobody does. These things were invented thousands of years ago, when the race still lived in barbarism. Each age has simply extended their usefulness and efficiency. So it is wrong to speak of any invention as the work of one man. Into every great invention go the experience and experiments of countless others.

So much for that side of the question. Now, let us look at another side of the question which is sometimes lost sight of. A man invents a machine: as I have shown you, it is as much the product of other men's brains as of his own. It is really a social product. He gets a patent upon the machine for a certain number of years, and that patent gives him the right to say to the world "No one can use this machine unless he pays me a royalty." He does not use the machine himself and keep what he can make in competition with others' means of production. If no one chooses to use his machine, then, no matter how good a thing it may be, he gets nothing from his invention. So that even the inventor is no exception to my statement that no man ever gets rich by his own labor.

The inventor is not the real inventor of the machine: he only carries on the work which others began thousands of years ago. He takes the results of other people's inventive genius and adds his quota. But he claims the whole. And when he has done his work and added his contribution to the age-long development of mechanical modes of production, he must depend again upon society, upon the labor of others.

To return to the question of abstinence: I would not attempt to deny that some men have saved part of their income and by investing it secured the beginnings of great fortunes. I know that is so. But the fortunes came out of the labor of other people. Somebody had to produce the wealth, that is quite evident. And if the person who got it was not that somebody, the producer, it is as clear as noonday that the producer must have produced something he did not get.

No, my friend, the notion that profits are the reward of abstinence and thrift is stupid in the extreme. The people who enjoy the profit-incomes of the world, are, with few exceptions, people who have not been either abstemious or thrifty.

But perhaps you will say that, while this may be true of the people who to-day are getting enormous incomes from rent, interest or profit, we must go further back; that we must go back to the beginning of things when their fathers or their grandfathers began by investing their savings.

To that I have no objection whatever, provided only that you are willing to go back, not merely to the beginning of the individual fortune, but to the beginning of the system. If your grandfather, or great-grandfather, had been what is termed a thrifty and industrious man, working hard, living poor, working his wife and little ones in one long grind, all in order to save money to invest in business, you might now be a rich man; that is, supposing you were heir to their possessions.

That is not at all certain, for it is a fact that most of the men who have hoarded their individual savings and then invested them have been ruined and fooled. In the case of our railroads, for example, the great majority of the early investors of savings went bankrupt. They were swallowed up by the bigger fish, Jonathan. But assume it otherwise, assume that the grandfather of some rich man of the present day laid the foundation of the family fortune in the manner described, don't you see that the system of robbing the worker of his product was already established; that you must go back to the beginning of the system?

And when you trace capital back to its origin, my friend, you will always come to war or robbery. You can trace it back to the forcible taking of the land away from the people. When the machine came, bringing with it an industrial revolution, it was by the wealthy and the ruthless that the machine was owned, not by the poor toilers. In other words, my friends, there was simply a continuance of the old rule of a class of overlords, under another name.

If the abstinence theory is foolish, even more foolish is the notion that profits are the reward of managing ability, the wages of superintendence. Under primitive capitalism there was some justification for this view.

It was impossible to deny that the owner of a factory did manage it, that he was the superintendent, entitled as such to some reward. It was easy enough to say that he got a disproportionate share, but who was to decide just what his fair share would be?

But when capitalism developed and became impersonal that idea of the nature of profits was killed. When companies were organized they employed salaried managers, whose salaries were paid before profits were reckoned at all. To-day I can own shares in China and Australia while living all the time in the United States. Even though I have never been to those countries, nor seen the property I am a shareholder in, I shall get my profits just the same. A lunatic may own shares in a thousand companies and, though he is confined in a madhouse, his shares of stock will still bring a profit to his guardians in his name.

When Mr. Rockefeller was summoned to court in Chicago last year, he stated on oath that he could not tell anything about the business of the Standard Oil Company, not having had anything to do with the business for several years past. But he gets his profits just the same, showing how foolish it is to talk of profits as being the reward of managing ability and the wages of superintendence.

Now, Jonathan, I have explained to you pretty fully what Socialism is when considered as a philosophy of social evolution. I have also explained to you what Socialism is when considered as a system of economy. I could sum up both very briefly by saying that Socialism is a philosophy of social evolution which teaches that the great force which has impelled the race onward, determining the rate and direction of social progress, has come from man's tools and the mode of production in general: that we are now living in a period of transition, from capitalism to Socialism, motived by the economic forces of our time. Socialism is a system of economics, also. Its substance may be summed up in a sentence as follows: Labor applied to natural resources is the source of the wealth of capitalistic society, but the greatest part of the wealth produced goes to non-producers, the producers getting only a part, in the form of wages--hence the paradox of wealthy non-producers and penurious producers.

I have explained to you also that Socialism is not a scheme. There remains still to be explained, however, another aspect of Socialism, of more immediate interest and importance and interest. I must try to explain Socialism as an ideal, as a forecast of the future. You want to know, having traced the evolution of society to a point where everything seems to be in transition, where a change seems imminent, just what the nature of that change will be.

I must leave that for another letter, friend Jonathan, for this is over-long already. I shall not try to paint a picture of the future for you, to tell you in detail what that future will be like. I do not know: no man can know. He who pretends to know is either a fool or a knave, my friend. But there are some things which, I believe, we may premise with reasonable certainty These things I want to discuss in my next letter. Meantime, there are lots of things in this letter to think about.

And I want you to think, Jonathan Edwards!

IX

WHAT SOCIALISM IS AND WHAT IT IS NOT

(Continued)

And the wolf shall dwell with the lamb, and the leopard shall lie down with the kid; and the calf and the young lion and the fattling together; and a little child shall lead them. And the cow and the bear shall feed; their young ones shall lie down together; and the lion shall eat straw like the ox. And the suckling child shall play on the hole of the asp, and the weaned child shall put his hand on the basilisk's den. They shall not hurt nor destroy in all my holy mountain: for the earth shall be full of the knowledge of the Lord, as the waters cover the sea.--Isaiah.

But we are not going to attain Socialism at one bound. The transition is going on all the time, and the important thing for us, in this explanation, is not to paint a picture of the future--which in any case would be useless labor--but to forecast a practical programme for the intermediate period, to formulate and justify measures that shall be applicable at once, and that will serve as aids to the new Socialist birth.--W. Liebknecht.

At the head of this letter I have copied two passages to which I want you to give particular attention, Jonathan. The first consists of a part of a very beautiful word-picture, in which the splendid old Hebrew prophet described his vision of a perfect social state. In his Utopia it would no longer be true to speak of Nature as being red of tooth and claw. Even the lion would eat straw like the ox, so that there might not be suffering caused by one animal preying upon another. Whenever I read that chapter, Jonathan, I sit watching the smoke-wreaths curl out of my pipe and float away, and they seem to bear me with them to a land of seductive beauty. I should like to live in a land where there was never a cry of pain, where never drop of blood stained the ground.

There have been lots of Utopias besides that of the old Hebrew prophet. Plato, the great philosopher, wrote The Republic to give form to his dream of an ideal society. Sir Thomas More, the great English statesman and martyr, outlined his ideal of social relations in a book called Utopia. Mr. Bellamy, in our own day, has given us his picture of social perfection in Looking Backward. There have been many others who, not content with writing down their ideas of what society ought to be like, have tried to establish ideal conditions. They have established colonies, communities, sects and brotherhoods, all in the earnest hope of being able to attain the perfect social state.

The greatest of these experimental Utopians, Robert Owen, tried to carry out his ideas in this country. It would be well worth your while to read the account of his life and work in George Browning Lockwood's book, The New Harmony Communities. Owen tried to get Congress to adopt his plans for social regeneration. He addressed the members of both houses, taking with him models, plans, diagrams and statistics, showing exactly how things would be, according to his idea, in the ideal world. In Europe he went round to all the reigning sovereigns begging them to adopt his plans.

He wanted common ownership of everything with equal distribution; money would be abolished; the marriage system would be done away with and "free love" established; children would belong to and be reared by the community. Our concern with him at this point is that he called himself a Socialist and was, I believe, the first to use that word.

But the Socialists of to-day have nothing in common with such Utopian ideas as those I have described. We all recognize that Robert Owen was a beautiful spirit, one of the world's greatest humanitarians. He was, like the prophet Isaiah, a dreamer, a visionary. He had no idea of the philosophy of social evolution upon which modern Socialism rests; no idea of its system of economics. He saw the evils of private ownership and competition in the fiercest period of competitive industry, and wanted to replace them with co-operation and public ownership. But his point of view was that he had been inspired with a great idea, thanks to which he could save the world from all its misery. He did not realize that social changes are produced by slow evolution.

One of the principal reasons why I have dwelt at this length upon Owen is that he is a splendid representative of the great Utopia builders. The fact that he was probably the first man to use the word Socialism adds an element of interest to his personality also. I wanted to put Utopian Socialism before you so clearly that you would be able to contrast it at once with modern, scientific Socialism--the Socialism of Marx and Engels, upon which the great Socialist parties of the world are based; the Socialism that is alive in the world to-day. They are as opposite as the poles. It is important that you should grasp this fact very clearly, for many of the criticisms of Socialism made to-day apply only to the old utopian ideals and do not touch modern Socialism at all. In the letter you wrote me at the beginning of this discussion there are many questions which you could not have asked had you not conceived of Socialism as a scheme to be adopted.

People are constantly attacking Socialism upon these false grounds. They remind me of a story I heard in Wales many years ago. In one of the mountain districts a miner returned from his work one afternoon and found that his wife had bought a picture of the crucifixion of Jesus and hung it against the wall. He had never heard of Jesus, so the story goes, and his wife had to explain the meaning of the picture. She told the story in her simple way, laying much stress upon the fact that "the wicked Jews" had killed Jesus. But she forgot to say that it all happened about two thousand years ago.

Now, it happened not long after that the miner saw a Jew peddler come to the door of his cottage. The thought of the awful suffering of Jesus and his own Welsh hatred of oppression sufficed to fill him with resentment toward the poor peddler. He at once began to beat the unfortunate fellow in a terribly savage manner. When the peddler, between gasps, demanded to know why he had been so ill-treated, the miner dragged him into his kitchen and pointed to the picture of the crucifixion. "See what you did to that poor man, our Lord!" he thundered. To which the Jew very naturally responded: "But, my friend, that was not me. That was two thousand years ago!" The reply seemed to daze the miner for a moment. Then he said: "Two thousand years! Two thousand years! Why, I only heard of it last week!"

It is just as silly to attack the Socialism of to-day for the ideas held by the earlier utopian Socialists as beating that poor Jew peddler was.

Now then, friend Jonathan, turn back and read the second of the passages I have placed at the head of this letter. It is from the writings of one of the greatest of modern Socialists, the man who was the great political leader of the Socialist movement in Germany, Wilhelm Liebknecht.

You will notice that he says the transition to Socialism is going on all the time; that we are not to attain Socialism at one bound; that it is useless to attempt to paint pictures of the future; that we can forecast an immediate programme and aid the Socialist birth. These statements are quite in harmony with the outline of the Socialist philosophy of the evolution of society contained in my last letter.

So, if you ask me to tell you just what the world will be like when all people call themselves Socialists except a few reformers and "fanatics," earnest pioneers of further changes, I must answer you that I do not know. How they will dress, what sort of pictures artists will paint, what sort of poems poets will write, or what sort of novels men and women will read, I do not know. What the income of each family will be I cannot tell you, any more than I can tell you whether there will be any intercommunication between the inhabitants of this planet and of Mars; whether there will be an ambassador from Mars at the national capital.

I do not expect that the lion will eat straw like the ox; I do not expect that people will be perfect. I do not suppose that men and women will have become so angelic that there will never be any crime, suffering, anger, pain or sorrow; I do not expect disease to be forever banished from life in the Socialist regime. Still less do I expect that mechanical genius will have been so perfected that human labor will be no longer necessary; that perpetual motion will have been harnessed to great indestructible machines and work become a thing of the past. That dream of the German dreamer, Etzler, will never be realized, I hope.

I suppose that, under Socialism, there will be some men and women far wiser than others. There may be a few fools left! I suppose that some will be far juster and kinder than others. There may be some selfish brutes left with a good deal of hoggishness in their nature! I suppose that some will have to make great mistakes and endure the tragedies which men and women have endured through all the ages. The love of some men will die out, breaking the hearts of some women, I suppose, and there will be women whose love will bring them to ruin and death. I should not like to think of jails and brothels existing under Socialism, Jonathan, but for all I know they may exist. Whether there will be churches and paid ministers under Socialism, I do not know. I do not pretend to know.

I suppose that, under Socialism, there will be some people who will be dissatisfied. I hope so! Men and women will want to move to a higher plane of life, I hope. What they will call that plane I do not know; what it will be like I do not know. I suppose they will be opposed and persecuted; that they will be mocked and derided, called "fanatics" and "dreamers" and lots of other ugly and unpleasant names. Lots of people will want to stay just as they are, and violently oppose the men who say, "Let us move on." But I don't believe that any sane person will want to go back to the old conditions--back to our conditions of to-day.

You see, I have killed lots of your objections already, my friend!

Now let me tell you briefly what Socialists want, and what they believe will take place--must take place. In the first place, there must be political changes to make complete our political democracy. You may be surprised at this, Jonathan. Perhaps you are accustomed to think of our political system as being the perfect expression of political democracy. Let us see.

Compared with some other countries, like Russia, Germany and Spain, for example, this is a free country, politically; a model of democracy. We have adult suffrage--for the men! In only a few states are our mothers, wives, sisters and daughters allowed to vote. In most of the states the best women, and the most intelligent, are placed on the political level of the criminal and the maniac. They must obey the laws, their interests in the well-being and good government of the nation are as vital as those of our sex. But they are denied representation in the councils of the nation, denied a voice in the affairs of the nation. They are not citizens. We have a class below that of the citizens in this country, a class based upon sex distinctions.

To make our political system thoroughly representative and democratic, we must extend political power to the women of the nation. Further than that, we must bring all the means of government more directly under the people's will.

In our industrial system we must bring the great trusts under the rule of the people. They must be owned and controlled by all for all. I say that we "must" do this, because there is no other way by which the present evils may be remedied. Everybody who is not blinded to the real situation by vested interest must recognize that the present conditions are intolerable--and becoming worse and more intolerable every day. A handful of men have the nation's destiny in their greedy fingers and they gamble with it for their own profit. Something must be done.

But what? We cannot go back if we would. I have shown you pretty clearly, I think, that if it were possible to undo the chain of evolution and to go back to primitive capitalism, with its competitive spirit, the development to monopoly would begin all over again. It is an inexorable law that competition breeds monopoly. So we cannot go back.

What, then, is the outlook, the forward view? So far as I know, Jonathan, there are only two propositions for meeting the evil conditions of monopoly, other than the perfectly silly one of "going back to competition." They are (1) Regulation of the trusts; (2) Socialization of the trusts.

Now, the first means that we should leave these great monopolies in the hands of their present owners and directors, but enact various laws curtailing their powers to exploit the people. Laws are to be passed limiting the capital they may employ, the amount of profits they may make, and so on. But nobody explains how they expect to get the laws obeyed. There are plenty of laws now aiming at regulation of the trusts, but they are quite futile and inoperative. First we spend an enormous amount of money and energy getting laws passed; then we spend much more money and energy trying to get them enforced--and fail after all!

I submit to your good judgment, Jonathan, that so long as we have a relatively small class in the nation owning these great monopolies through corporations there can be no peace. It will be to the interest of the corporations to look after their profits, to prevent the enactment of legislation aimed to restrict them and to evade the law as much as possible. They will naturally use their influence to secure laws favorable to themselves, with the inevitable result of corruption in the legislative branches of the government. Legislators will be bought like mackerel in the market, as Mr. Lawson so bluntly expresses it. Efforts will be made to corrupt the judiciary also and the power of the entire capitalist class will be directed to the capture of our whole system of government. Even more than to-day, we will have the government of the people by a privileged part of the people in the interests of the privileged part.

You must not forget, my friend, that the corruption of the government about which we hear so much from time to time is always in the interests of private capitalism. If there is graft in some public department, there is an outcry that graft and public business go together. As a matter of fact the graft is in the interests of private capitalism.

When legislators sell their votes it is never for public enterprises. I have never heard of a city which was seeking the power to establish any public service raising a "yellow dog fund" with which to bribe legislators. On the other hand, I never yet heard of a private company seeking a franchise without doing so more or less openly. Regulation of the trusts will still leave the few masters of the many, and corruption still gnawing at the vitals of the nation.

We must own the trusts, Jonathan, and transform the monopolies by which the few exploit and oppress the many into social monopolies for the good of all. Sooner or later, either by violent or peaceful means, this will be done. It is for the working-class to say whether it shall be sooner or later, whether it shall be accomplished through the strife and bitterness of war or by the peaceful methods of political conquest.

We have seen that the root of the evil in modern society is the profit motive. Socialism means the production of things for use instead of for profit. Not at one stroke, perhaps, but patiently, wisely and surely, all the things upon which people in common depend will be made common property.

Take notice of that last paragraph, Jonathan. I don't say that all property must be owned in common, but only the things upon which people in common depend; the things which all must use if they are to live as they ought, and as they have a right to live. We have a splendid illustration of social property in our public streets. These are necessary to all. It would be intolerable if one man should own the streets of a city and charge all other citizens for the use of them. So streets are built out of the common funds, maintained out of the common funds, freely used by all in common, and the poorest man has as much right to use them as the richest man. In the nutshell this states the argument of Socialism.

People sometimes ask how it would be possible for the government under Socialism to decide which children should be educated to be writers, musicians and artists and which to be street cleaners and laborers; how it would be possible to have a government own everything, deciding what people should wear, what food should be produced, and so on.

The answer to all such questions is that Socialism would not need to do anything of the kind. There would be no need for the government to attempt such an impossible task. When people raise such questions they are thinking of the old and dead utopianism, of the schemes which once went under the name of Socialism. But modern Socialism is a principle, not a scheme. The Socialist movement of to-day is not interested in carrying out a great design, but in seeing society get rid of its drones and making it impossible for one class to exploit another class.

Under Socialism, then, it would not be at all necessary for the government to own everything; for private property to be destroyed. For instance, the State could have no possible interest in denying the right of a man to own his home and to make that home as beautiful as he pleased. It is perfectly absurd to suppose that it would be necessary to "take away the poor man's cottage," about which some opponents of Socialism shriek. It would not be necessary to take away anybody's home.

On the contrary, Socialism would most likely enable all who so desired to own their own homes. At present only thirty-one per cent. of the families of America live in homes which they own outright. More than half of the people live in rented homes. They are obliged to give up practically a fourth part of their total income for mere shelter.

Socialism would not prevent a man from owning a horse and wagon, since it would be possible for him to use that horse and wagon without compelling the citizens to pay tribute to him. On the other hand, private ownership of a railway would be impossible, because railways could not be indefinitely and easily multiplied, and the owners of such a railway would necessarily have to run it for profit.

Under Socialism such public services as the transportation and delivery of parcels would be in the hands of the people, and not in the hands of monopolists as at present. The aim would be to serve the people to the best possible advantage, and not to make profit for the few. But if any citizen objected and wanted to carry his own parcel from New York to Boston, for example, it is not to be supposed for an instant that the State would try to prevent him.

Under Socialism the great factories would belong to the people; the trusts would be socialized. But this would not stop a man from working for himself in a small workshop if he wanted to; it would not prevent a number of workers from forming a co-operative workshop and sharing the products of their labor. By reason of the fact that the great productive and distributive agencies which are entirely social were socially owned and controlled-- railways, mines, telephones, telegraphs, express service, and the great factories of various kinds--the Socialist State would be able to set the standards of wages and industrial conditions for all the rest remaining in private hands.

Let me explain what I mean, Jonathan: Under Socialism, let us suppose, the State undertakes the production of shoes by socializing the shoe trust. It takes over the great factories and runs them. Its object is not to make shoes for profit, however, but for use. To make shoes as good as possible, as cheaply as good shoes can be made, and to see that the people making the shoes get the best possible conditions of labor and the highest possible wages--as near as possible to the net value of their product, that is.

Some people, however, object to wearing factory-made shoes; they want shoes of a special kind, to suit their individual fancy. There are also, we will suppose, some shoemakers who do not like to work in the State factories, preferring to make shoes by hand to suit individual tastes. Now, if the people who want the handmade shoes are willing to pay the shoemakers as much as they could earn in the socialized factories no reasonable objection could be urged against it. If they would not pay that amount, or near it, the shoemakers, it is reasonable to suppose, would not want to work for them. It would adjust itself.

Under Socialism the land would belong to the people. By this I do not mean that the private use of land would be forbidden, because that would be impossible. There would be no object in taking away the small farms from their owners. On the contrary, the number of such farms might be greatly increased. There are many people to-day who would like to have small farms if they could only get a fair chance, if the railroads and trusts of one kind and another were not always sucking all the juice from the orange. Socialism would make it possible for the farmer to get what he could produce, without having to divide up with the railroad companies, the owners of grain elevators, money-lenders, and a host of other parasites.

I have no doubt, Jonathan, that under Socialism there would be many privately-worked farms. Nor have I any doubt whatever that the farmers would be much better off than under existing conditions. For to-day the farmer is not the happy, independent man he is sometimes supposed to be. Very often his lot is worse than that of the city wage-earner. At any rate, the money return for his labor is often less. You know that a great many farmers do not own their farms: they are mortgaged and the farmer has to pay an average interest of six per cent. upon the mortgage.

Now, let us look for a moment at such a farmer's conditions, as shown by the census statistics. According to the census of 1900, there were in the United States 5,737,372 farms, each averaging about 146 acres. The total value of farm products in 1899 was $4,717,069,973. Now then, if we divide the value of the products by the number of farms, we can get the average annual product of each farm--about $770.

Out of that $770 the farmer has to pay a hired laborer for at least six months in the year, let us say. At twenty-five dollars a month, with an added eight dollars a month for his board, this costs the farmer $198, so that his income now stands at $572. Next, he must pay interest upon his mortgage at six per cent. per annum. Now, the average value of the farms in 1899 was $3,562 and six per cent. on that amount would be about $213. Subtract that sum from the $572 which the farmer has after paying his hired man and you have left about $356. But as the farms are, not mortgaged to their full value, suppose we reduce the interest one half--the farmer's income remains now $464.

Now, as a general thing, the farmer and his wife have to work equally hard, and they must work every day in the year. The hired laborer gets $150 and his board for six months, at the rate of $300 and board per year. The farmer and his wife get only $232 a year each and part of their board, for what is not produced on the farm they must buy.

Under Socialism the farmer could own his own farm to all intents and purposes. While the final title might be vested in the government, the farmer would have a title to the use of the farm which no one could dispute or take from him. If he had to borrow money he would do it from the government and would not be charged extortionate rates of interest as he is now. He would not have to pay railroad companies' profits, since the railways being owned by all for all and not run for profit, would be operated upon a basis of the cost of service. The farmer would not be exploited by the packers and middlemen, these functions being assumed by the people through their government, upon the same basis of service to all, things being done for the use and welfare of all instead of for the profit of the few. Under Socialism, moreover, the farmer could get his machinery from the government factories at a price which included no profits for idle shareholders.

I am told, Jonathan, that at the present time it costs about $24 to make a reaper which the farmer must pay $120 for. It costs $40 to sell the machine which was made for $24, the expense being incurred by wasteful and useless advertising, salesmen's commissions, travelling expenses, and so on. The other $54 which the farmer must pay goes to the idlers in the form of rent, interest and profit.

Socialism, then, could very well leave the farmer in full possession of his farm and improve his position by making it possible for him to get the full value of his labor-products without having to divide up with a host of idlers and non-producers. Socialism would not deny any man the use of the land, but it would take away the right of non-users to reap the fruits of the toil of users. It would deny the right of the Astor family to levy a tax upon the people of New York, amounting to millions of dollars annually, for the privilege of living there. The Astors have such a vast business collecting this tax that they have to employ an agent whose salary is equal to that of the President of the United States and a large army of employees.

Socialism would deny the right of the English Duke of Rutland and Lord Beresford to hold millions of acres of land in Texas, and to levy a tax upon Americans for its use. It would deny the right of the British Land Company to tax Kansans for the use of the 300,000 acres owned by the company; the right of the Duke of Sutherland and Sir Edward Reid to tax Americans for the use of the millions of acres they own in Florida; of Lady Gordon and the Marquis of Dalhousie to any right to tax people in Mississippi. The idea that a few people can own the land upon which all people must live in any country is a relic of slavery, friend Jonathan.

So you see, my friend, Socialism does not mean that everything is to be divided up equally among the people every little while. That is either a fool's notion or the wilful misrepresentation of a liar. Socialism does not mean that there is to be a great bureaucratic government owning everything and controlling everybody. It does not mean doing away with private initiative and making of humanity a great herd, everybody wearing the same kind of clothes, eating the same kind and quantities of food, and having no personal liberties. It simply means that all men and women should have equal opportunities; to make it impossible for one man to exploit another, except at that other's free will. It does not mean doing away with individual liberty and reducing all to a dead level. That is what is at present happening to the great majority of people, and Socialism comes to unbind the soul of man--to make mankind free.

I think, Jonathan, that you ought to have a fairly clear notion now of what Socialism is and what it is not. You ought to be able now to distinguish between the social properties which Socialism would establish and the private properties it could have no object in taking away, which it would rather foster and protect. I have tried simply to illustrate the principle for you, so that you can think the matter out for yourself. It will be a very good thing for you to commit this rule to memory.--

Under Socialism, the State would own and control only those things which could not be owned and controlled by individuals without giving them an undue advantage over the community, by enabling them to extract profits from the labor of others.

But be sure that you do not make the common mistake of confusing government ownership with Socialism, friend Jonathan, as so many people are in the habit of doing. In Prussia the government owns the railways. But the government does not represent the interests of all the people. It is the government of a nation by a class. That is not the same thing as the socialization of the railways, as you will see. In Russia the government owns some of the railways and has a monopoly of the liquor traffic. But these things are not democratically owned and managed in the common interest. Russia is an autocracy. Everything is run for the benefit of the governing class, the Czar and a host of bureaucrats. That is not Socialism. In this country we have a nearer approach to democracy in our government, and our post-office system, for example, is a much nearer approach to the realization of the Socialist principle.

But even in this country, government ownership and Socialism are not the same thing. For our government is a class government too. There is the same inequality of wages and conditions as under capitalist ownership: many of the letter carriers and other employees are miserably underpaid, and the service is notoriously handicapped by private interests. Whether it is in Russia under the Czar and his bureaucrats, Germany with its monarchial system cumbered with the remnants of feudalism, or the United States with its manhood suffrage foolishly used to elect the interests of the capitalist class, government ownership can only be at best a framework for Socialism. It must wait for the Socialist spirit to be infused into it.

Socialists want government ownership, Jonathan, but they don't want it unless the people are to own the government. When the government represents the interests of all the people it will use the things it owns and controls for the common good. And that will be Socialism in practice, my friend.

X

OBJECTIONS TO SOCIALISM CONSIDERED

I feel sure that the time will come when people will find it difficult to believe that a rich community such as our's, having such command over external nature, could have submitted to live such a mean, shabby, dirty life as we do.--William Morris.

Morality and political economy unite in repelling the individual who consumes without producing.--Balzac.

The restraints of Communism would be freedom in comparison with the present condition of the majority of the human race.--John Stuart Mill.

I promised at the beginning of this discussion, friend Jonathan, that I would try to answer the numerous objections to Socialism which you set forth in your letter, and I cannot close the discussion without fulfilling that promise.

Many of the objections I have already disposed of and need not, therefore, take further notice of them here. The remaining ones I propose to answer-- except where I can show you that an answer is unnecessary. For you have answered some of the objections yourself, my friend, though you were not aware of the fact. I find in looking over the long list of your objections that one excludes another very often. You seem, like a great many other people, to have set down all the objections you had ever heard, or could think of at the time, regardless of the fact that they could not by any possibility be all well founded; that if some were wise and weighty others must be foolish and empty. Without altering the form of your objections, simply rearranging their order, I propose to set forth a few of the contradictions in your objections. That is fair logic, Jonathan.

First you say that you object to Socialism because it is "the clamor of envious men to take by force what does not belong to them." That is a very serious objection, if true. But you say a little further on in your letter that "Socialism is a noble and beautiful dream which human beings are not perfect enough to realize in actual life." Either one of the objections may be valid, Jonathan, but both of them cannot be. Socialism cannot be both a noble and a beautiful dream, too sublime for human realization, and at the same time a sordid envy--can it?

You say that "Socialists are opposed to law and order and want to do away with all government," and then you say in another objection that "Socialists want to make us all slaves to the government by putting everything and everybody under government control." It happens that you are wrong in both assertions, but you can see for yourself that you couldn't possibly be right in both of them--can't you?

You object that under Socialism "all would be reduced to the same dead level." That is a very serious objection, too, but it cannot be well founded unless your other objection, that "under Socialism a few politicians would get all the power and most of the wealth, making all the people their slaves" is without foundation. Both objections cannot hold--can they?

You say that "Socialists are visionaries with cut and dried schemes that look well on paper, but the world has never paid any attention to schemes for reorganizing society," and then you object that "the Socialists have no definite plans for what they propose to do, and how they mean to do it; that they indulge in vague principles only." And I ask you again, friend Jonathan, do you think that both these objections can be sound?

You object that "Socialism is as old as the world; has been tried many times and always failed." If that were true it would be a very serious objection to Socialism, of course. But is it true? In another place you object that "Socialism has never been tried and we don't know how it would work." You see, my friend, you can make either objection you choose, but not both. Either one may be right, but both cannot be.

Now, these are only a few of the long list of your objections which are directly contradictory and mutually exclusive, my friend. Some of them I have already answered directly, the others I have answered indirectly. Therefore, I shall do no more here and now than briefly summarize the Socialist answer to them.

Socialists do propose that society as a whole should take and use for the common good some things which a few now own, things which "belong" to them by virtue of laws which set the interests of the few above the common good. But that is a very different thing from "the clamor of envious men to take what does not belong to them." It is no more to be so described than taxation, for example is. Socialism is a beautiful dream in one sense. Men who see the misery and despair produced by capitalism think with joy of the days to come when the misery and despair are replaced by gladsomeness and hope. That is a dream, but no Socialist rests upon the dream merely: the hope of the Socialist is in the very material fact of the economic development from competition to monopoly; in the breakdown of capitalism itself.

You have probably learned by this time that Socialism does not mean either doing away with all government or making the government master of everything. Later, I want to return to the subject, and to the charge that it would reduce all to a dull level. I shall not waste time answering the objections that it is a scheme and that it is not a scheme, further than I have already answered them. And I am not going to waste your time arguing at length the folly of saying that Socialism has been tried and proved a failure. The Socialism of to-day has nothing to do with the thousands of Utopian schemes which men have tried. Before the modern Socialist movement came into existence, during hundreds of years, men and women tried to realize social equality by forming communities and withdrawing from the ordinary life of the world. Some of these communities, mostly of a religious nature, such as the Shakers and the Perfectionists, attained some measure of success and lasted a number of years, but most of them lasted only a short time. It is folly to say that Socialism has ever been tried anywhere at any time.

And now, friend Jonathan, I want to consider some of the more vital and important objections to Socialism made in your letter. You object to Socialism

Because its advocates use violent speech Because it is "the same as Anarchism" Because it aims to destroy the family and the home Because it is opposed to religion Because it would do away with personal liberty Because it would reduce all to one dull level Because it would destroy the incentive to progress Because it is impossible unless we can change human nature.

These are all your objections, Jonathan, and I am going to try to suggest answers to them.

(1) It is true that Socialists sometimes use very violent language. Like all earnest and enthusiastic men who are possessed by a great and overwhelming sense of wrong and needless suffering, they sometimes use language that is terrible in its vehemence; their speech is sometimes full of bitter scorn and burning indignation. It is also true that their speech is sometimes rough and uncultured, shocking the sensitive ear, but I am sure you will agree with me that the working man or woman who, never having had the advantage of education and refined environment, feels the burden of the days that are or the inspiration of better days to come, is entitled to be heard. So I am not going to apologize for the rough and uncultured speech.

And I am not going to apologize for the violent speech. It would be better, of course, if all the advocates of Socialism could master the difficult art of stating their case strongly and without compromise, but without bitterness and without unnecessary offense to others. But it is not easy to measure speech in the denunciation of immeasurable wrong, and some of the greatest utterances in history have been hard, bitter, vehement words torn from agonized hearts. It is true that Socialists now and then use violent language, but no Socialist--unless he is so overwrought as to be momentarily irresponsible--advocates violence. The great urge and passion of Socialism is for the peaceful transformation of society.

I have heard a few overwrought Socialists, all of them gentle and generous comrades, incapable of doing harm to any living creature, in bursts of tempestuous indignation use language which seemed to incite their hearers to violence, but those who heard them understood that they were borne away by their feelings. I have never heard Socialists advocate violence toward any human beings in cold-blooded deliberation. But I have heard capitalists and the defenders of capitalism advocate violence toward Socialists in cold-blooded deliberation. I have seen in Socialist papers upon a few occasions violent utterances which I deplored, but never such advocacy of violence as I have read in newspapers opposed to Socialism. Here, for example, are some extracts from an editorial which appeared January, 1908, in the columns of the Gossip, of Goldfield, Nevada:

"A cheaper and more satisfactory method of dealing with this labor trouble in Goldfield last spring would have been to have taken half a dozen of the Socialist leaders in the Miners' Union and hanged them all to telegraph poles.

"SPEAKING DISPASSIONATELY, AND WITHOUT ANIMUS, it seems clear to us after many months of reflection, that YOU COULDN'T MAKE A MISTAKE IN HANGING A SOCIALIST.

"HE IS ALWAYS BETTER DEAD.

"He, breathing peace, breathing order, breathing goodwill, fairness to all and moderation, is always the man with the dynamite. He is the trouble-maker, and the trouble-breeder.

"To fully appreciate him you must live where he abounds.

"In the Western Federation of Miners he is that plentiful legacy left us from the teachings of Eugene V. Debs, hero of the Chicago Haymarket Riots.

"ALWAYS HANG A SOCIALIST. NOT BECAUSE HE'S A DEEP THINKER, BUT BECAUSE HE'S A BAD ACTOR."

I could fill many pages with extracts almost as bad as the above, all taken from capitalist papers, Jonathan. But for our purpose one is as good as a thousand. I want you to read the papers carefully with an eye to their class character. When the Goldfield paper printed the foregoing open incitement to murder, the community was already disturbed by a great strike and the President of the United States had sent federal troops to Goldfield in the interest of the master class. Suppose that under similar circumstances a

Socialist paper had come out and said in big type that people "couldn't make a mistake in hanging a capitalist," that capitalists are "always better dead." Suppose that any Socialist paper urged the murder of Republicans and Democrats in the same way, do you think the paper would have been tolerated? That the editor would have escaped jail? Don't you know that if such a statement had been published by any Socialist paper the whole country would have been roused, that press and pulpit would have denounced it?

Socialists are opposed to violence. They appeal to brains and not to bludgeons; they trust in ballots and not in bullets. The violence of speech with which they are charged is not the advocacy of violence, but unmeasured and impassioned denunciation of a cruel and brutal system. Not long ago I heard a clergyman denouncing Socialists for their "violent language." Poor fellow! He was quite unconscious that he was more bitter in his invective than the men he attacked. Of course Socialists use bitter and burning language--but not more bitter than was used by the great Hebrew prophets in their stern denunciations; not more bitter than was used by Jesus and his disciples; not more bitter than was used by Martin Luther and other great leaders of the Reformation; not more bitter than was used by Garrison and the other Abolitionists. Men with vital messages cannot always use soft words, Jonathan.

(2) Socialism is not "the same as Anarchism," my friend, but its very opposite. The only connection between them is that they are agreed upon certain criticisms of present society. In all else they are as opposite as the poles. The difference lies not merely in the fact that most Anarchists have advocated physical violence, for there are some Anarchists who are as much opposed to physical violence as you or I, Jonathan, and it is only fair and just that we should recognize the fact. It has always seemed to me that Anarchism logically leads to physical force by individuals against individuals, but, logical or no, there are many Anarchists who are gentle spirits, holding all life sacred and abhorring violence and assassination. When there are so many ready to be unjust to them, we can afford to be just to the Anarchists, even if we do

not agree with them, Jonathan.

Sometimes an attempt is made by Socialists to explain the difference between themselves and Anarchists by saying that Anarchists want to destroy all government, while Socialists want to extend government and bring everything under its control; that Anarchists want no laws, while Socialists want more laws. But that is not an intelligent statement of the difference. We Socialists don't particularly desire to extend the functions of government; we are not so enamoured of laws that we want more of them. Quite the contrary is true, in fact. If we had a Socialist government to-morrow in this country, one of the first and most important of its tasks would be to repeal a great many of the existing laws.

Then there are some Socialists who try to explain the difference between Socialism and Anarchism by saying that the Anarchists are simply Socialists of a very advanced type; that society must first pass through a period of Socialism, in which laws will be necessary, before it can enter upon Anarchism, a state in which every man will be so pure and so good that he can be a law unto himself, no other form of law being necessary. But that does not settle the difficulty. I think you will see, friend Jonathan, that in order to have such a society in which without laws or penal codes, or government of any kind, men and women lived happily together, it would be necessary for every member to cultivate a social sense, a sense of responsibility to society as a whole. Each member of society would have to become so thoroughly socialized as to make the interests of society as a whole his chief concern in life. And such a society would be simply a Socialist society perfectly developed, not an Anarchist society. It would be a Socialist society simply because it would be dominated by the essential principle of Socialism--the idea of solidarity, of common interest.

The basis of Anarchism is utopian individualism. Just as the old utopian dreamers who tried to "establish" Socialism through the medium of numerous "Colonies," took the abstract idea of equality and made it their ideal, so the Anarchist sets up the abstract idea of individual liberty. The true difference between Socialism and Anarchism is that the Socialist sets the social interest, the good of society, above all other interests, while the Anarchist sets the interest of the individual above everything else. You could express the difference thus:

Socialism means We -ism Anarchism means Me -ism

The Anarchist says: "The world is made up of individuals. What is called "society" is only a lot of individuals. Therefore the individual is the only real being and society a mere abstraction, a name. As an individual I know myself, but I know nothing of society; I know my own interests, but I know nothing of what you call the interests of society." On the other hand, the Socialist says that "no man liveth unto himself," to use a biblical phrase. He points out that in modern society no individual life, apart from the social life, is possible.

If this seems a somewhat abstract way of putting it, Jonathan, just try to put it in a concrete form yourself by means of a simple experiment. When you sit down to your breakfast to-morrow morning take time to think where your breakfast came from and how it was produced. Think of the coffee plantations in far-off countries drawn on for your breakfast; of the farms, perhaps thousands of miles away, from which came your bacon and your bread; of the coal miners toiling that your breakfast might be cooked; of the men in the engine-rooms of great ships and on the tenders of mighty locomotives, bringing your breakfast supplies across sea and land. Then think of your clothing in the same way, article by article, trying to realize how much you are dependent upon others than yourself. Throughout the day apply the same principle as you move about. Apply it to the streets as you go to work; to the street cars as you ride; apply it to the provisions which are made to safeguard your health against devastating plague, the elaborate system of drainage, the carefully guarded water-supply, and so on. Then, when you have done that for a day as far as possible, ask yourself whether the Anarchist idea that every individual is a distinct and separate whole, an independent being, unrelated to the other individuals who make up society, is a true one; or whether the Socialist idea that all individuals are inter-dependent upon each other, bound to each other by so many ties that they cannot be considered apart, is the true idea. Judge by your experience, Jonathan!

So the Socialist says that "we are all members one of another," to use another familiar biblical phrase. He is not less interested in personal freedom than the Anarchist, not less desirous of giving to each individual unit in society the largest possible freedom compatible with the like freedom of all the other units. But, while the Anarchist says that the best judge of that is the individual, the Socialist says that society is the best judge. The Anarchist position is that, in the event of a conflict of interests, the will of the individual must rule at all costs; the Socialist says that, in the event of such a conflict of interests, the will of the individual must give way. That is the real philosophical difference between the two.

Anarchism is not important enough in America, friend Jonathan, to justify our devoting so much time and space to the discussion of its philosophy as opposed to the philosophy of Socialism, except for the bearing it has upon the political movement of the working class. I want you to see just how Anarchism works out when the test of practical application is resorted to.

Just as the Anarchist sets up an abstract idea of individual liberty as his ideal, so he sets up an abstract idea of tyranny. To him Law, the will of society, is the essence of tyranny. Laws are limitations of individual liberty set by society and therefore they are tyrannical. No matter what the law may be, all laws are wrong. There cannot be such a thing as a good law, according to this view. To illustrate just where this leads us, let me tell of a recent experience: I was lecturing in a New England town, and after the lecture an Anarchist rose to ask some questions. He wanted to know if it was not a fact that all laws were oppressive and bad, to which, of course, I replied that I thought not.

I asked him whether the law forbidding murder and providing for its punishment, oppressed him; whether he felt it a hardship not to be allowed to murder at will, and he replied that he did not. I cited many other laws, such as the laws relating to arson, burglary, criminal assault, and so on, with the same result. His outcry about the oppression of law, as such, proved to be just an empty cry about an abstraction; a bogey of his imagination. Of course, he could cite bad laws, unjust laws, as I could have done; but that would simply show that some laws are not right--a proposition upon which most people will agree. My Anarchist friend quoted Herbert Spencer in support of his contention. He referred to Spencer's well-known summary of the social legislation of England. So I asked my friend if he thought the Factory Acts were oppressive and tyrannical, and he replied that, from an Anarchist viewpoint, they were.

Think of that, Jonathan! Little boys and girls, five and six years old, were taken out of their beds crying and begging to be allowed to sleep, and carried to the factory gates. Then they were driven to work by brutal overseers armed with leather whips. Sometimes they fell asleep at their tasks and then they were beaten and kicked and cursed at like dogs. Little boys and girls from orphan asylums were sent to work thus, and died like flies in summer-- their bodies being secretly buried at night for fear of an outcry. You can find the terrible story told in The Industrial History of England, by H. de B. Gibbins, which ought to be in your public library.

Humane men set up a protest at last and there was a movement through the country demanding protection for the children. Once a member of parliament held up in the House of Commons a whip of leather thongs attached to an oak handle, telling his colleagues that a few days before it had been used to flog little children who were mere babies. The demand was made for legislation to stop this barbarous treatment of children, to protect their childhood. The factory owners opposed the passing of such laws on the ground that it would be an interference with their individual liberties, their right to do as they pleased. And the Anarchist comes always and inevitably to the same conclusion. Factory laws, public health laws, education laws--all denounced as "interferences with individual liberty." Extremes meet: the Anarchist in the name of individual liberty, like the capitalist, would prevent society from putting a stop to the exploitation of its little ones.

The real danger in Anarchism is not that some Anarchists believe in violence, and that from time to time there are cowardly assassinations which are as futile as they are cowardly. The real danger lies first in the reactionary principle that the interests of society must be subordinated to the interests of the individual, and, second, in holding out a hope to the working class that its freedom from oppression and exploitation may be brought about by other than political, legislative means. And it is this second objection which is of extreme importance to the working class of America at this time.

From time to time, in all working class movements, there is an outcry against political action, an outcry raised by impetuous men-in-a-hurry who want twelve o'clock at eleven. They cry out that the ballot is too slow; they want some more "direct" action than the ballot-box allows. But you will find, Jonathan, that the men who raise this cry have nothing to propose except riot to take the place of political action. Either they would have the workers give up all struggle and depend upon moral suasion, or they would have them riot. And we Socialists say that ballots are better weapons than bullets for the workers. You may depend upon it that any agitation among the workers against the use of political weapons leads to Anarchism--and to riot. I hope you will find time to read Plechanoff's Anarchism and Socialism, Jonathan. It will well repay your careful study.

No, Socialism is not related to Anarchism, but it is, on the contrary, the one great active force in the world to-day that is combating Anarchism. There is a close affinity between Anarchism and the idea of capitalism, for both place the individual above society. The Socialist believes that the highest good of the individual will be realized through the highest good of society.

(3) Socialism involves no attack upon the family and the home. Those who raise this objection against Socialism charge that it is one of the aims of the Socialist movement to do away with the monogamic marriage and to replace it with what is called "Free Love." By this term they do not really mean free love at all. For love is always free, Jonathan. Not all the wealth of a Rockefeller could buy one single touch of love. Love is always free; it cannot

be bought and it cannot be bound. No one can love for a price, or in obedience to laws or threats. The term "Free Love" is therefore a misnomer.

What the opponents of Socialism have in mind when they use the term is rather lust than love. They charge us Socialists with trying to do away with the monogamic marriage relation--the marriage of one man to one woman-- and the family life resulting therefrom. They say that we want promiscuous sex relations, communal life instead of family life and the turning over of all parental functions to the community, the State. And to charge that these things are involved in Socialism is at once absurd and untrue. I venture to say, Jonathan, that the percentage of Socialists who believe in such things is not greater than the percentage of Christians believing in them, or the percentage of Republicans or Democrats. They have nothing to do with Socialism.

Let us see upon what sort of evidence the charge is based: On the one hand, finding nothing in the programmes of the Socialist parties of the world to support the charge, we find them going back to the utopian schemes with communistic features. They go back to Plato, even! Because Plato in his Republic, which was a wholly imaginary description of the ideal society he conceived in his mind, advocated community of sex relations as well as community of goods, therefore the Socialists, who do not advocate community of goods or community of wives, must be charged with Plato's principles! In like manner, the fact that many other communistic experiments included either communism of sex relations, as, for example, the Adamites, during the Hussite wars, in Germany, and the Perfectionists, of Oneida, with their "community marriage," all the male members of a community being married to all the female members; or enforced celibacy, as did the Shakers and the Harmonists, among many other similar groups, is urged against Socialism.

I need not argue the injustice and the stupidity of this sort of criticism, Jonathan. What have the Socialists of twentieth century America to do with Plato? His utopian ideal is not their ideal; they are neither aiming at community of goods nor at community of wives. And when we put aside Plato and the Platonic communities, the first fact to challenge attention is that the communities which established laws relating to sex relations which were opposed to the monogamic family, whether promiscuity, so-called free love; plural marriage, as in Mormonism, or celibacy, as in Harmonism and Shakerism, were all religious communities. In a word, all these experiments which antagonized the monogamic family relation were the result of various interpretations of the Bible and the efforts of those who accepted those interpretations to rule their lives in accordance therewith. In every case communism was only a means to an end, a way of realizing what they considered to be the true religious life. In other words, my friend, most of the so-called free love experiments made in these communities have been offshoots of Christianity rather than of Socialism.

And I ask you, Jonathan Edwards, as a fair-minded American, what you would think of it if the Socialists charged Christianity with being opposed to the family and the home? It would not be true of Christianity and it is not true of Socialism.

But there is another form of argument which is sometimes resorted to. The history of the movement is searched for examples of what is called free love. That is to say that because from time to time there have been individual Socialists who have refused to recognize the ceremonial and legal aspects of marriage, believing love to be the only real marriage bond, notwithstanding that the vast majority of Socialists have recognized the legal and ceremonial aspects of marriage, they have been accused of trying to do away with marriage. Our opponents have even stooped so low as to seize upon every case where Socialists have sought divorce as a means of undoing terrible wrong, and then married other husbands and wives, and proclaimed it as a fresh proof that Socialism is opposed to marriage and the family. When I have read some of these cruel and dishonest attacks, often written by men who know better, my soul has been sickened at the thought of the cowardice and dishonesty to which the opponents of Socialism resort.

Suppose that every time a prominent Christian becomes divorced, and then remarries, the Socialists of the country were to attack the Christian religion and the Christian churches, upon the ground that they are opposed to marriage and the family, does anybody think that that would be fair and just? But it is the very thing which happens whenever Socialists are divorced. It happened, not so very long ago, that a case of the kind was made the occasion of hundreds of editorials against Socialism and hundreds of sermons. The facts were these: A man and his wife, both Socialists, had for a long time realized that their marriage was an unhappy one. Failing to realize the happiness they sought, it was mutually agreed that the wife should apply for a divorce. They had been legally married and desired to be legally separated. Meantime the man had come to believe that his happiness depended upon his wedding another woman. The divorce was to be procured as speedily as possible to enable the legal marriage of the man and the woman he had grown to love.

Those were the facts as they appeared in the press, the facts upon which so many hundreds of attacks were made upon Socialism and the Socialist movement. Two or three weeks later, an Episcopal clergyman, not a Socialist, left the wife he had ceased to love and with whom he had presumably not been happy. He had legally married his wife, but he did not bother about getting a legal separation. He just left his wife; just ran away. He not only did not bother about getting a legal separation, but he ran away with a young girl, whom he had grown to love. They lived together as man and wife, without legal marriage, for if they went through any marriage form at all it was not a legal marriage and the man was guilty of bigamy. Was there any attack upon the Episcopal Church in consequence? Were hundreds of sermons preached and editorials written to denounce the church to which he belonged, accusing it of aiming to do away with the monogamic marriage relation, to break up the family and the home?

Not a bit of it, Jonathan. There were some criticisms of the man, but there were more attempts to find excuses for him. There were thousands of expressions of sympathy with his church. But there were no attacks such as were aimed at Socialism in the other case, notwithstanding that the Socialist strictly obeyed the law whereas the clergyman broke the law and defied it. I think that was a fair way to treat the case, but I ask the same fair treatment of Socialism.

So far, Jonathan, I have been taking a defensive attitude, just replying to the charge that Socialism is an attack upon the family and the home. Now, I want to go a step further: I want to take an affirmative position and to say that Socialism comes as the defender of the home and the family; that capitalism from the very first has been attacking the home. I am going to turn the tables, Jonathan.

When capitalism began, when it came with its steam engine and its power-loom, what was the first thing it did? Why, it entered the home and took the child from the mother and made it a part of a great system of wheels and levers and springs, all driven for one end--the grinding of profit. It began its career by breaking down the bonds between mother and child. Then it took another step. It took the mother away from the baby in the cradle in order that she too might become part of the great profit-grinding system. Her breasts might be full to overflowing with the food wonderfully provided for the child by Nature; the baby in the cradle might cry for the very food that was bursting from its mother's breasts, but Capital did not care. The mother was taken away from the child and the child was left to get on as best it might upon a miserable substitute for its mother's milk. Hundreds of thousands of babies die each year for no other reason than this.

There will never be safety for the home and the family so long as babies are robbed of their mothers' care; so long as little children are made to do the work of men; so long as the girls who are to be the wives and mothers are sent into wifehood and motherhood unprepared, simply because the years of maidenhood are spent in factories that ought to be spent in preparation for wifehood and motherhood. Here is capitalism cutting at the very heart of the home, with Socialism as the only defender of the home it is charged with attacking. For Socialism would give the child its right to childhood; it would give the mother her freedom to nourish her babe; it would give to the fathers and mothers of the future the opportunities for preparation they cannot now enjoy.

I ask you, friend Jonathan, to think of the tens and thousands of women who marry to-day, not because they love and are loved in return, but for the sake of getting a home. Socialism would put an end to that condition by making woman economically and politically free. Think of the tens of thousands of young men in our land who do not, dare not, marry because they have no certainty of earning a living adequate to the maintenance of wives and families; of the hundreds of thousands of prostitutes in our country, the vast majority of whom have been driven to that terrible fate by economic causes outside of their control. Socialism would at least remove the economic pressure which forces so many of these women down into the terrible hell of prostitution. I ask you, Jonathan, to think also of the thousands of wives who are deserted every year. So far as the investigations of the charity organizations into this serious matter have gone, it has been shown that poverty is responsible for by far the greatest number of these desertions. Socialism would not only destroy the poverty, but it would set woman economically free, thus removing the main causes of the evil.

Oh, Jonathan Edwards, hard-headed, practical Jonathan, do you think that the existence of the family depends upon keeping women in the position of an inferior class, politically and economically? Do you think that when women are politically and economically the equals of men, so that they no longer have to marry for homes, or to stand brutal treatment because they have no other homes than the men afford; so that no woman is forced to sell her body--I ask you, when women are thus free do you believe that the marriage system will be endangered thereby? For that is what the contention of the opponents of Socialism comes to in the last analysis, my friend. Socialism will only affect the marriage system in so far as it raises the standards of society as a whole and makes woman man's political and economic equal. Are you afraid of that, Jonathan?

(4) Socialism is not opposed to religion. It is perfectly true that some Socialists oppose religion, but Socialism itself has nothing to do with matters of religion. In the Socialist movement to-day there are men and women of all creeds and all shades of religious belief. By all the Socialist parties of the world religion is declared to be a private matter--and the declaration is honestly meant; it is not a tactical utterance, used as bait to the unwary, which the Socialists secretly repudiate. In the Socialist movement of America to-day there are Jews and Christians, Catholics and Protestants, Spiritualists and Christian Scientists, Unitarians and Trinitarians, Methodists and Baptists, Atheists and Agnostics, all united in one great comradeship.

This was not always the case. When the scientific Socialist movement began in the second half of the last century, Science was engaged in a great intellectual encounter with Dogma. All the younger men were drawn into the scientific current of the time. It was natural, then, that the most radical movement of the time should partake of the universal scientific spirit and temper. The Christians of that day thought that the work of Darwin and his school would destroy religion. They made the very natural mistake of supposing that dogma and religion were the same thing, a mistake which their critics fully shared.

You know what happened, Jonathan. The Christians gradually came to realize that no religion could oppose the truth and continue to be a power. Gradually they accepted the position of the Darwinian critics, until to-day there is no longer the great vital controversy upon matters of theology which our fathers knew. In a very similar manner, the present generation of Socialists have nothing to do with the attacks upon religion which the Socialists of fifty years ago indulged in. The position of all the Socialist parties of the world to-day is that they have nothing to do with matters of religious belief; that these belong to the individual alone.

There is a sense in which Socialism becomes the handmaiden of religion: not of creeds and theological beliefs, but of religion in its broadest sense. When you examine the great religions of the world, Jonathan, you will find that in addition to certain supernatural beliefs there are always great ethical principles which constitute the most vital elements in religion. Putting aside the theological beliefs about God and the immortality of the soul, what was it that gave Judaism its power? Was it not the ethical teaching of its great prophets, such as Isaiah, Joel, Amos and Ezekiel--the stern rebuke of the oppressors of the poor and downtrodden, the scathing denunciation of the despoilers of the people, the great vision of a unified world in which there should be peace, when war should no more blight the world and when the weapons of war should be forged into plowshares and pruning hooks? Leaving matters of theology aside, are not these the principles which make Judaism a living religion to-day for so many? And I say to you, Jonathan, that Socialism is not only not opposed to these things, but they can only be realized under Socialism.

So with Christianity. In its broadest sense, leaving aside all matters of a supernatural character, concerning ourselves only with the relation of the religion to life, to its material problems, we find in Christianity the same great faith in the coming of universal peace and brotherhood, the same defense of the poor and the oppressed, the same scathing rebuke of the oppressor, that we find in Judaism. There is the same relentless scourge of the despoilers, of those who devour widows houses. And again I say that Socialism is not only not opposed to the great social ideals of Christianity, but it is the only means whereby they may be realized. And the same thing is true of the teachings of Confucius; Buddha and Mahomet. The great social ideals common to all the world's religions can never be attained under capitalism. Not till the Socialist state is reached will the Golden Rule, common to all the great religions, be possible as a rule of life. No ethical life is possible except as the outgrowing of just and harmonic economic relations; until it is rooted in proper economic soil.

No, Jonathan, it is not true that Socialism is antagonistic to religion. With beliefs and speculations concerning the origin of the universe it has nothing to do. It has nothing to do with speculations concerning the existence of man after physical death, with belief in the immortality of the soul. These are for the individual. Socialism concerns itself with man's material life and his relation to his fellow man. And there is nothing in the philosophy of Socialism, or the platform of the political Socialist movement, antagonistic to the social aspects of any religion.

(5) I have already had a good deal to say in the course of this discussion concerning the subject of personal freedom. The common idea of Socialism as a great bureaucratic government owning and controlling everything, deciding what every man and woman must do, is wholly wrong. The aim and purpose of the Socialist movement is to make life more free for the individual, and not to make it less free. Socialism means equality of opportunity for every child born into the world; it means doing away with class privilege; it means doing away with the ownership by the few of the things upon which the lives of the many depend, through which the many are exploited by the few. Do you see how individuals are to be enslaved through the destruction of the power of a few over many, Jonathan? Think it out!

It is in the private ownership of social resources, and the private control of social opportunities, that the essence of tyranny lies. Let me ask you, my friend, whether you feel yourself robbed of any part of your personal liberty when you go to a public library and take out a book to read, or into one of our public art galleries to look upon great pictures which you could never otherwise see? Is it not rather a fact that your life is thereby enriched and broadened; that instead of taking anything from you these things add to your enjoyment and to your power? Do you feel that you are robbed of any element of your personal freedom through the action of the city government in making parks for your recreation, providing hospitals to care for you in case of accident or illness, maintaining a fire department to protect you against the ravages of fire? Do you feel that in maintaining schools, baths, hospitals, parks, museums, public lighting service, water, streets and street cleaning service, the city government is taking away your personal liberties? I ask these questions, Jonathan, for the reason that all these things contain the elements of Socialism.

When you go into a government post-office and pay two cents for the service of having a letter carried right across the country, knowing that every person must pay the same as you and can enjoy the same right as you, do you feel that you are less free than when you go into an express company's office and pay the price they demand for taking your package? Does it really help you to enjoy yourself, to feel yourself more free, to know that in the case of the express company's service only part of your money will be used to pay the cost of carrying the package; that the larger part will go to bribe legislators, to corrupt public officials and to build up huge fortunes for a few investors? The post-office is not a perfect example of Socialism: there are too many private grafters battening upon the postal system, the railway companies plunder it and the great mass of the clerks and carriers are underpaid. But so far as the principles of social organization and equal charges for everybody go they are socialistic. The government does not try to compel you to write letters any more than the private company tries to compel you to send packages. If you said that, rather than use the postal system, you would carry your own letter across the continent, even if you decided to walk all the way, the government would not try to stop you, any more than the express company would try to stop you from carrying your trunk on your shoulder across the country. But in the case of the express company you must pay tribute to men who have been shrewd enough to exploit a social necessity for their private gain.

Do you really imagine, Jonathan, that in those cities where the street railways, for example, are in the hands of the people there is a loss of personal liberty as a result; that because the people who use the street railways do not have to pay tribute to a corporation they are less free than they would otherwise be? So far as these things are owned by the people and democratically managed in the interests of all, they are socialistic and an appeal to such concrete facts as these is far better than any amount of abstract reasoning. You are not a closet philosopher, interested in fine-spun theories, but a practical man, graduated from the great school of hard experience. For you, if I am not mistaken, Garfield's aphorism, that "An ounce of fact is worth many tons of theory," is true.

So I want to ask you finally concerning this question of personal liberty whether you think you would be less free than you are to-day if your Pittsburg foundries and mills, instead of belonging to corporations organized for the purpose of making profit, belonged to the Commonwealth of Pennsylvania, and if they were operated for the common good instead of as now to serve the interests of a few. Would you be less free if, instead of a corporation trying to make the workers toil as many hours as possible for as little pay as possible, naturally and consistently avoiding as far as possible the expenditure of time and money upon safety appliances and other means of protecting the health and lives of the workers, the mills were operated upon the principle of guarding the health and lives of the workers as much as possible, reducing the hours of labor to a minimum and paying them for their work as much as possible? Is it a sensible fear, my friend, that the people of any country will be less free as they acquire more power over their own lives? You see, Jonathan, I want you to take a practical view of the matter.

(6) The cry that Socialism would reduce all men and women to one dull level is another bogey which frightens a great many good and wise people. It has been answered thousands of times by Socialist writers and you will find it discussed in most of the popular books and pamphlets published in the interest of the Socialist propaganda. I shall therefore dismiss it very briefly.

Like many other objections, this rests upon an entire misapprehension of what Socialism really means. The people who make it have got firmly into their minds the idea that Socialism aims to make all men equal; to devise some plan for removing the inequalities with which they are endowed by nature. They fear that, in order to realize this ideal of equality, the strong will be held down to the level of the weak, the daring to the level of the timid, the wisest to the level of the least wise. That is their conception of the equality of which Socialists talk. And I am free to say, Jonathan, that I do not wonder that sensible men should oppose such equality as that.

Even if it were possible, through the adoption of some system of stirpiculture, to breed all human beings to a common type, so that they would all be tall or short, fat or thin, light or dark, according to choice, it would not be a very desirable ideal, would it? And if we could get everybody to think exactly the same thoughts, to admire exactly the same things, to have exactly the same mental powers and exactly the same measure of moral strength and weakness, I do not think that would be a very desirable ideal. The world of human beings would then be just as dull and uninspiring as a waxwork show. Imagine yourself in a city where every house was exactly like every other house in all particulars, even to its furnishings; imagine all the people being exactly the same height and weight, looking exactly alike, dressed exactly alike, eating exactly alike, going to bed and rising at the same time, thinking exactly alike and feeling exactly alike--how would you like to live in such a city, Jonathan? The city or state of Absolute Equality is only a fool's dream.

No sane man or woman wants absolute equality, friend Jonathan, for it is as undesirable as it is unimaginable. What Socialism wants is equality of opportunity merely. No Socialist wants to pull down the strong to the level of the weak, the wise to the level of the less wise. Socialism does not imply pulling anybody down. It does not imply a great plain of humanity with no mountain peaks of genius or character. It is not opposed to natural inequalities, but only to man-made inequalities. Its only protest is against these artificial inequalities, products of man's ignorance and greed. It does not aim to pull down the highest, but to lift up the lowest; it does not want to put a load of disadvantage upon the strong and gifted, but it wants to take off the heavy burdens of disadvantage which keep others from rising. In a word, Socialism implies nothing more than giving every child born into the world equal opportunities, so that only the inequalities of Nature remain. Don't you believe in that, my friend?

Here are two babies, just born into the world. Wee, helpless seedlings of humanity, they are wonderfully alike in their helplessness. One lies in a tenement upon a mean bed, the other in a mansion upon a bed of wonderful richness. But if they were both removed to the same surroundings it would be impossible to tell one from the other. It has happened, you know, that babies have been mixed up in this way, the child of a poor servant girl taking the place of the child of a countess. Scientists tell us that Nature is wonderfully democratic, and that, at the moment of birth, there is no physical difference between the babies of the richest and the babies of the poorest. It is only afterward that man-made inequalities of conditions and opportunities make such a wide difference between them.

Look at our two babies a moment: no man can tell what infinite possibilities lie behind those mystery-laden eyes. It may be that we are looking upon a future Newton and another Savonarola, or upon a greater than Edison and a greater than Lincoln. No man knows what infinitude of good or ill is germinating back of those little puckered brows, nor which of the cries may develop into a voice that will set the hearts of men aflame and stir them to glorious deeds. Or it may be that both are of the common clay, that neither will be more than an average man, representing the common level in physical and mental equipment.

But I ask you, friend Jonathan, is it less than justice to demand equal opportunities for both? Is it fair that one child shall be carefully nurtured amid healthful surroundings, and given a chance to develop all that is in him, and that the other shall be cradled in poverty, neglected, poorly nurtured in a poor hovel where pestilence lingers, and denied an opportunity to develop physically, mentally and morally? Is it right to watch and tend one of the human seedlings and to neglect the other? If, by chance of Nature's inscrutable working, the babe of the tenement came into the world endowed with the greater possibilities of the two, if the tenement mother upon her mean bed bore into the world in her agony a spark of divine fire of genius, the soul of an artist like Leonardo da Vinci, or of a poet like Keats, is it less than a calamity that it should die--choked by conditions which only ignorance and greed have produced?

Give all the children of men equal opportunities, leaving only the inequalities of Nature to manifest themselves, and there will be no need to fear a dull level of humanity. There will be hewers of wood and drawers of water content to do the work they can; there will be scientists and inventors, forever enlarging man's kingdom in the universe; there will be makers of songs and dreamers of dreams, to inspire the world. Socialism wants to unbind the souls of men, setting them free for the highest and best that is in them.

Do you know the story of Prometheus, friend Jonathan? It is, of course, a myth, but it serves as an illustration of my present point. Prometheus, for ridiculing the gods, was bound to a rock upon Mount Caucasus, by order of Jupiter, where daily for thirty years a vulture came and tore at his liver, feeding upon it. Then there came to his aid Hercules, who unbound the tortured victim and set him free. Like another Prometheus, the soul of man to-day is bound to a rock--the rock of capitalism. The vulture of Greed tears the victim, remorselessly and unceasingly. And now, to break the chains, to set the soul of man free, Hercules comes in the form of the Socialist movement. It is nothing less than this; my friend. In the last analysis, it is the bondage of the soul which counts for most in our indictment of capitalism and the liberation of the soul is the goal toward which we are striving.

It is to-day, under capitalism, that men are reduced to a dull level. The great mass of the people live dull, sordid lives, their individuality relentlessly crushed out. The modern workman has no chance to express any individuality in his work, for he is part of a great machine, as much so as any one of the many levers and cogs. Capitalism makes humanity appear as a great plain with a few peaks immense distances apart--a dull level of mental and moral attainment with a few giants. I say to you in all seriousness, Jonathan, that if nothing better were possible I should want to pray with the poet Browning,--

Make no more giants, God-- But elevate the race at once!

But I don't believe that. I am satisfied that when we destroy man-made inequalities, leaving only the inequalities of Nature's making, there will be no need to fear the dull level of life. When all the chains of ignorance and greed have been struck from the Prometheus-like human soul, then, and not till then, will the soul of man be free to soar upward.

(7) For the reasons already indicated, Socialism would not destroy the incentive to progress. It is possible that a stagnation would result from any attempt to establish absolute equality such as I have already described. If it were the aim of Socialism to stamp out all individuality, this objection would be well founded, it seems to me. But that is not the aim of Socialism.

The people who make this objection seem to think that the only incentive to progress comes from a few men and their hope and desire to be masters of the lives of others, but that is not true. Greed is certainly a powerful incentive to some kinds of progress, but the history of the world shows that there are other and nobler incentives. The hope of getting somebody else's property is a powerful incentive to the burglar and has led to the invention of all kinds of tools and ingenious methods, but we do not hesitate to take away that incentive to that kind of "progress." The hope of getting power to exploit the people acts as a powerful incentive to great corporations to devise schemes to defeat the laws of the nation, to corrupt legislators and judges, and otherwise assail the liberties of the people. That, also, is "progress" of a kind, but we do not hesitate to try to take away that incentive.

Even to-day, Jonathan, Greed is not the most powerful incentive in the world. The greatest statesmanship in the world is not inspired by greed, but by love of country, the desire for the approbation and confidence of others, and numerous other motives. Greed never inspired a great teacher, a great artist, a great scientist, a great inventor, a great soldier, a great writer, a great poet, a great physician, a great scholar or a great statesman. Love of country, love of fame, love of beauty, love of doing, love of humanity--all these have meant infinitely more than greed in the progress of the world.

(8) Finally, Jonathan, I want to consider your objection that Socialism is impossible until human nature is changed. It is an old objection which crops up in every discussion of Socialism. People talk about "human nature" as

though it were something fixed and definite; as if there were certain quantities of various qualities and instincts in every human being, and that these never changed from age to age. The primitive savage in many lands went out to seek a wife armed with a club. He hunted the woman of his choice as he would hunt a beast, capturing and clubbing her into submission. That was human nature, Jonathan. The modern man in civilized countries, when he goes seeking a wife, hunts the woman of his choice with flattery, bon-bons, flowers, opera tickets and honeyed words. Instead of a brute clubbing a woman almost to death, we see the pleading lover, cautiously and earnestly wooing his bride. And that, too, is human nature. The African savages suffering from the dread "Sleeping Sickness" and the poor Indian ryots suffering from Bubonic Plague see their fellows dying by thousands and think angry gods are punishing them. All they can hope to do is to appease the gods by gifts or by mutilating their own poor bodies. That is human nature, my friend. But a great scientist like Dr. Koch, of Berlin, goes into the African centres of pestilence and death, seeks the germ of the disease, drains swamps, purifies water, isolates the infected cases and proves himself more powerful than the poor natives' gods. And that is human nature. Outside the gates of the Chicago stockyards, I have seen crowds of men fighting for work as hungry dogs fight over a bone. That was human nature. I have seen a man run down in the streets and at once there was a crowd ready to lift him up and to do anything for him that they could. It was the very opposite spirit to that shown by the brutish, snarling, cursing, fighting men at the stockyards, but it was just as much human nature.

The great law of human development, that which expresses itself in what is so vaguely termed human nature, is that man is a creature of his environment, that self-preservation is a fundamental instinct in human beings. Socialism is not an idealistic attempt to substitute some other law of life for that of self-preservation. On the contrary, it rests entirely upon that instinct of self-preservation. Here are two classes opposed to each other in modern society. One class is small but exceedingly powerful, so that, despite its disadvantage in size, it is the ruling class, controlling the larger class and exploiting it. When we ask ourselves how that is possible, how it happens that the smaller class rules the larger, we soon find that the members of the smaller class have become conscious of their interests and the fact that these can be best promoted through organization and association. Thus conscious of their class interests, and acting together by a class instinct, they have been able to rule the world. But the workers, the class that is much stronger numerically, have been slower to recognize their class interests. Inevitably, however, they are developing a similar class sense, or instinct. Uniting in the economic struggle at first, and then, in the political struggle in order that they may further their economic interests through the channels of government, it is easy to see that only one outcome of the struggle is possible. By sheer force of numbers, the workers must win, Jonathan.

The Socialist movement, then, is not something foreign to human nature, but it is an inevitable part of the development of human society. The fundamental instinct of the human species makes the Socialist movement inevitable and irresistible. Socialism does not require a change in human nature, but human nature does require a change in society. And that change is Socialism. It is perhaps the deepest and profoundest instinct in human beings that they are forever striving to secure the largest possible material comfort, forever striving to secure more of good in return for less of ill. And in that lies the great hope of the future, Jonathan. The great Demos is learning that poverty is unnecessary, that there is plenty for all; that none need suffer want; that it is possible to suffer less and to live more; to have more of good while suffering less of ill. The face of Demos is turned toward the future, toward the dawning of Socialism.

XI

WHAT TO DO

Are you in earnest? Seize this very minute. What you can do, or dream you can, begin it! Boldness has genius, power and magic in it. Only engage and then the mind grows heated; Begin, and then the work will be completed.--Goethe.

Apart from those convulsive upheavals that escape all forecast and are sometimes the final supreme resource of history brought to bay, there is only one sovereign method for Socialism--the conquest of a legal majority.--Jean Jaur 鑛.

When one is convinced of the justice and wisdom of the Socialist idea, when its inspiration has begun to quicken the pulse and to stir the soul, it is natural that one should desire to do something to express one's convictions and to add something, however little, to the movement. Not only that, but the first impulse is to seek the comradeship of other Socialists and to work with them for the realization of the Socialist ideal.

Of course, the first duty of every sincere believer in Socialism is to vote for it. No matter how hopeless the contest may seem, nor how far distant the electoral triumph, the first duty is to vote for Socialism. If you believe in Socialism, my friend, even though your vote should be the only Socialist vote in your city, you could not be true to yourself and to your faith and vote any other ticket. I know that it requires courage to do this sometimes. I know that there are many who will deride the action and say that you are "wasting your vote," but no vote is ever wasted when it is cast for a principle, Jonathan. For, after all, what is a vote? Is it not an expression of the citizen's conviction concerning the sort of government he desires? How, then can his vote be thrown away if it really expresses his conviction? He is entitled to a single voice, and provided that he avails himself of his right to declare through the ballot box his conviction, no matter whether he stands alone or with ten thousand, his vote is not thrown away.

The only vote that is wasted is the vote that is cast for something other than the voter's earnest conviction, the vote of cowardice and compromise. The man who votes for what he fully believes in, even if he is the only one so voting, does not lose his vote, waste it or use it unwisely. The only use of a vote is to declare the kind of government the voter believes in. But the man who votes for something he does not want, for something less than his convictions, that man loses his vote or throws it away, even though he votes on the winning side. Get this well into your mind, friend Jonathan, for there are cities in which the Socialists would sweep everything before them and be elected to power if all the people who believe in Socialism, but refuse to vote for it on the ground that they would be throwing away their votes, would be true to themselves and vote according to their inmost convictions.

I say that we must vote for Socialism, Jonathan, because I believe that, in this country at least, the change from capitalism must be brought about through patient and wise political action. I have no doubt that the economic organizations, the trade unions, will help, and I can even conceive the possibility of their being the chief agencies in the transformation in society. That possibility, however, seems exceedingly remote, while the possibility of effecting the change through the ballot box is undeniable. Once let the working-class of America make up its mind to vote for Socialism, nothing can prevent its coming. And unless the workers are wise enough and united enough to vote together for Socialism, Jonathan, it is scarcely likely that they will be able to adopt other methods with success.

But as voting for Socialism is the most obvious duty of all who are convinced of its justness and wisdom, so it is the least duty. To cast your vote for Socialism is the very least contribution to the movement which you can make. The next step is to spread the light, to proclaim the principles of Socialism to others. To be a Socialist is the first step; to make Socialists is the second step. Every Socialist ought to be a missionary for the great cause. By talking with your friends and by circulating suitable Socialist literature, you can do effective work for the cause, work not less effective than that of the orator addressing big audiences. Don't forget, my friend, that in the Socialist movement there is work for you to do.

Naturally, you will want to be an efficient worker for Socialism, to be able to work successfully. Therefore you will need to join the organized movement, to become a member of the Socialist Party. In this way, working with many other comrades, you will be able to accomplish much more than as an individual working alone. So I ask you to join the party, friend Jonathan, and to assume a fair and just share of the responsibilities of the movement.

In the Socialist party organization there are no "Leaders" in the sense in which that term is used in connection with the political parties of capitalism. There are men who by virtue of long service and exceptional talents of various kinds are looked up to by their comrades, and whose words carry great weight. But the government of the organization is in the hands of the rank and file and everything is directed from the bottom upwards, not from the top downwards. The party is not owned by a few people who provide its funds, for these are provided by the entire membership. Each member of the party pays a small monthly fee, and the amounts thus contributed are divided between the local, state and national divisions of the organization. It is thus a party of the people, by the people and for the people, which bosses cannot corrupt or betray.

So I would urge you, Jonathan, and all who believe in Socialism, to join the party organization. Get into the movement in earnest and try to keep posted upon all that relates to it. Read some of the papers published by the party--at least two papers representing different phases of the movement. There are, always and everywhere, at least two distinct tendencies in the Socialist movement, a radical wing and a more moderate wing. Whichever of these appeals to you as the right tendency, you will need to keep informed as to both.

Above all, my friend, I would like to have you study Socialism. I don't mean merely that you should read a Socialist propaganda paper or two, or a few pamphlets: I do not call that studying Socialism. Such papers and pamphlets are very good in their way; they are written for people who are not Socialists for the purpose of awakening their interest. So far as they go they are valuable, but I would not have you stop there, Jonathan. I would like to have you push your studies beyond them, beyond even the more elaborate discussions of the subject contained in such books as this. Read the great classics of Socialist literature--and don't be afraid of reading the attacks made upon Socialism by its opponents. Study the philosophy of Socialism and its economic theories; try to apply them to your personal experience and to the events of every day as they are reported in the great newspapers. You see, Jonathan, I not only want you to know what Socialism is in a very thorough manner, but I also want you to be able to teach others in a very thorough manner.

And now, my patient friend, Good Bye! If The Common Sense of Socialism has helped you to a clear understanding of Socialism, I shall be amply repaid for writing it. I ask you to accept it for whatever measure of good it may do and to forgive its shortcomings. Others might have written a better book for you, and some day I may do better myself--I do not know. I have honestly tried my best to set the claims of Socialism before you in plain language and with comradely spirit. And if it succeeds in convincing you and making you a Socialist, Jonathan, I shall be satisfied.

* * * * *